Secret
Everybo

Wherever you are is the Entry Point.

 Kabir ⨾

Secrets of Astrology
Everybody Must Know

By

Dr. S.S. Gola

M.Com, Jyotish Martund,
Jyotish Ratan, Jyotish Kovid
Patron, Astro Science Research Organisation
President - Shri Sankat Mochan Ashram

Gullybaba Publishing House Pvt. Ltd

2525/193, 1st Floor, Onkar Nagar-A, Tri Nagar, Delhi-35
Landmark: Kanhaiya Nagar Metro Station
Tel.: 27387998, e-mail: info@gullybaba.com
Website: www.GullyBaba.com
www.AstrologyS.in

Secrets of Astrology Everybody Must Know

by *Dr. S.S. Gola*

Edition: 2012
Price: Rs.160/-

Copyright© 2012, Publisher

Develop and Produced by **Gullybaba Publishing House Pvt. Ltd**

Dedicated
**to all the readers who want to enhance their
quality through Astrology Science...**

Preface

In writing this book, it is tried to avoid making it too technical, in spite of the fact that it is an extremely complex subject. The main objective is to give readers an interesting into some of the fascinating intriguing and mysterious aspects of the oldest science known to mankind – Astrology. The main thrust was on the observation of various phenomena. Our sages were not mere spiritualists but matchless scientists of yesteryears they were a perfect blend of science and occult science (of which astrology is a part). Knowledge of astrology is incomplete without the knowledge of science. For many years we thought about unrevealing links between various sciences. This thought brought about enormous changes in handling of astrological problems.

This book will be an eye opener not only for astrologist but for others too. In astrological field most of the astrologers do not know science. Those who know science do not know astrology. Those who know both have not tried to bind it. Here a try is given to trace the missing links between various sciences – physics, chemistry, biology, alchemy, etc. – and astrology.

Astrology is the most difficult of all sciences. For drawing accurate conclusions one has to study the anatomy of the body together with the functions of the body and interpretation of these according to modern science. Study of physics, chemistry, biology, physiology, psychology, and philosophy is as necessary for an astrologer as for a scientist. This will definitely help the astrologer if he tries of trace links between astrology phenomena and modern science dealing with that aspect.

To conclude, it is a sincere hope that within these pages you will find something to inform you, entertain you, benefit you to bring a smile on your face and help you to gain a better understanding of yourself, family and friends. Constructive criticism is always welcome as it will add to knowledge.

- Dr. S.S. Gola

Acknowledgement

My sincere thanks to Sh. L.D. Madan, Sh. Nimai Banerjee. Mrs. Madhu Gola and Ms. Hemamalini editor of Express Star Teller Chennai for their whole hearted support extended to me in various capacities, without their help this book would not have seen the light of the day. My sincere thanks are for Dr. Charu Lata M.D. who guided me on various occassions regarding medicinal aspect without which the exact physical property of a planet would be a mystery. Also Mr. Dinesh Veerma author of "....And A Star is Born." the opening book selected by NBT, India and staff of the publisher (Gullybaba Publishing House Pvt. Ltd.) who are directly or indirectly related to this endeavour.

-Dr. S.S. Gola

Contents

Preface		*vii*
Acknowledgement		*ix*
1.	**What is Astrology?**	1
2.	**History of Astrology**	7
3.	**Psychology vs. Astrology**	13
	(Based on Sun sign)	
4.	**Planets in the Sky and their different conditions**	19
	(An accurate scientific understanding of Planets and its effect on us)	
5.	**Signs**	61
	(Based on Scientific and Mathematical Calculations)	
6.	**House**	73
	(Mathematical Calculated)	
7.	**Aspect**	77
8.	**Rationality in Sequence of Days**	79
	(An accurate scientific understanding of Planets and its effect on us)	
9.	**Significator**	83
	(Astrological Significator for good fortune)	
10.	**A Brief Description of Astronomical Terms**	85
	(Based on rising and setting of Particular Stars)	
11.	**Rahu and Undiagnosed Disease**	89
	(By modern Physics)	
12.	**Functional Benefics and Malefics**	93
	(As per Indian Vedic Astrology)	
13.	**Strength of Planet**	101
	(Based on Planetary Science)	

14.   **Principle for Interpretation**   **107**

15.   **Political Astrology**   **113**
       (Effect of Kundali on Politicians)

16.   **Sub-Sub-Period and Transit**   **125**

17.   **Astral Remedies**   **135**
       (For preventive as well as curative measures)

CHAPTER 1

What is Astrology?

Astrology is a science which has come down in us as a gift from the ancient Rishi. Rishi in Sanskrit means Inventor. In ancient India, Rishis were living in the forest amidst pollution free atmosphere. This noiseless atmosphere is still required for a scientific investigation. They had their scientific laboratories and visualised the effects of these stars/planet on animate and inanimate object and the star gazing could be better in a pollution free environment. They were constantly watching the movements of different planet. In those days, all the disciples required to study this science. These principles, which were laid down during that period still hold good but with passage of time, many important links were lost. As such a time came when anyone who knows little about the astrology was regarded as an astrologer.

According to the dictionary "Astrology is the science of the influence of the stars on human beings." Astrology is derived from the word. 'Aster' which means star and 'logos' which means logic or reason. In Sanskrit it is called Jyotish or the science of "Time". It attempts to foretell the history and also the future of man, fate of nations, empires, war, revolutions and many more. Astrology is a branch of Veda and is regarded as Vedanta (part of Vedas) with the help of which it is possible to tell all the past and future events by considering the ascendant and the planets at birth or at the time of posing a query.

Emerson has said:

"Astrology is excellent, but it must come up into life to have its full value, and not remain there as Globes and Spaces."

There are conflicting views on acceptance of astrology as a science. Those who do not believe have not studied astrology as a science. On account of the lack of knowledge, they criticise it.

Astrology is such a science that if utilised with patience, honesty and skill, it breaks through the barrier which separates life from the future and gives an insight into man's endeavours and his intimate destiny.

The Great astrologer Varahmihir in his monumental works 'Brahd Samhita' said 'A good astrologer must be able to explain question put by others, should worship the devas, observe fast & penance and should be able to suggest astral remedies. He should also be thoroughly trained in calculations of the positions of planets.

The cosmic science of astrology covers a wide field. It has three main branches:

1.   Siddhanta

2.   Samhita

3.   Hora Shastra

1. *Siddhanta:* It describes the method for determining the position of heavenly bodies in their transition. It deals with astronomy. The following have contributed much to this:

Pitamah, Surya, Vrihaspati, Manu, Atri, Vashist, Pulstya, Lomesh, Poulisa, Angira, Marchi, Vyas, Narad, Shaunk, Bhrigu, Chayvan, Kashyap, Garga, Parashar.

In astronomical science five school of thought are popular:

— Surya Siddhanta

— Romka (Lomesh) Siddhanta

— Paulisa Siddhanta

— Vashist Siddhanta

— Pitamah Siddhanta

2. Samhita: It describes rules for making weather forecast, rise or fall in commodities and agricultural products, epidemics, storms and political events, it has the following sub branches:

(a) Astro Meterology: A systematic study of the metrological science was made by our ancient astronomers and astrologers. It was taken up by Hindus as the branch of astrology because the heavenly bodies aspects, conjunctions etc. are all common to both. Every member of the solar system, which includes earth also, exert an important influence by way of gravitational force upon each other. All the planets exert control over the weather variations. But Mercury is the main planet. (This has been discussed at length in the author's other book on the subject.)

(b) Mundane Astrologer: This gives knowledge to predict important events which a country will pass through i.e. wars. earthquake, financial improvement or crisis, losses, fire, floods to famine etc. The effects of planets over the affairs of a nation are found to be just as powerful as they are over the life of an individual. These have been discussed in Author's book "Significant Mundane Events Through Transit Navasma."

3. Hora Shastra:

(a) **Natal Astrology:** It concerns largely with the life span of human beings. A chart is made out corresponding to the birth and with reference to the particular place of birth. From this chart, we can read all events in the life of a person, his nature, temperament, peculiarities, longevity, health, accident, finance, marriage, children, adversity etc. It is as useful for a king as for a layman.

(b) **Medical Astrology :** It is concerned with the aspect of health. All of us know that health is wealth. Money can purchase many things, but not everything. Health cannot be purchased by money. God may bless someone with money but he may not be enjoying good health. In the absence of the knowledge of astrology, a physician will rely on the trial and error method. If we know astrology we can identify the part of the body affected, detect the disease and also select opportune time for treatment. Hippocrates known as "Father of Medicine" has stated "A physician cannot safely administer medicine if he is not acquainted with astrology.

(c) **Horary Astrology :** This branch of science is also perfect, wonderful and most useful. With the aid of different principles one can offer correct, clear and precise prediction. Horary is derived from the word Hora. This is based on the questions raised by the querant. Whenever any querant comes we note the time and draw the chart based on that time and give the responses. Some astrologers ask the querant to give any number within 108. This number gives the basis for prediction. This is specially useful for those who do not have the details to constuct a horoscope.

(d) Electional /Muhurta Astrology : This is the branch of astrology which takes into account the most auspicious time for commencing any new undertaking for marriage, purchase of costly articles, construction of a house, time of getting admission in hospital, purchase of car etc.

(e) Kerala Astrology : The query is replied to by asking a person to touch any part of his body or asking the querant to mention the name of the flower.

CHAPTER 2

History of Astrology

The History of Astrology begins with the creation of this universe itself. Sage Garge says that this science was propounded by the Creation and Brahma handed it down to the sages at the time of Creation.

In Western countries there is a certain belief that Seth (3769 BC) was the world's first astrologer who studied the planets, their motions and their pathway. He divided the zodiac into 12 equal parts.

Around 2600 years ago, the priests of Chaldean took up this science for serious study and developed it. Their period was called the Golden Age of astrology, because they connected the movement of planets with all kinds of events in human life.

There is a second opinion that astrology had its origin in Chalden from times immemorial. The very name 'Chalden' means 'Astrologer' The Chaldeans who practiced this art of astrology were held in high esteem even at the time of Alexander the Great. Pathagoreans further advanced the concept of Chaldeans. They applied higher mathematics. Later astrology came into the hands of the Greeks. They concentrated more on Natal Astrology. They compiled horoscopes for the time of birth and could tell family background and the future of an individual. The British museum has in its collection of horoscope which is more than 2000 years old.

Egyptians were equally interested in astrology and they used astrology practically to shape the future of the nation. If we see the inscriptions on monuments this science goes back to 5000 BC. The Pharahos respected astrologers especially Babilus who was leader. He was always consulted and his responsibility was to tell how to expose the hidden enemies of the King. He used to interpret the dreams of the king. In Persia, the King used to honour the astrologers because of their sound knowledge of this science. They used the word "Al Hakim" which means astrologer. Sarasns spread this science in Spain in 411 AD and North Africans, the Moors in 1237 carried this science to Europe.

In China as far as 2752 BC from the days of King Fohi, Chinese developed astronomy to study astrology and Emperors were chosen by astrologers. In 2513 BC, Cheuni was elected the King is this manner, Henry Cornelius Agrippa (born 1486) was an astrologer to Francis the first Ruler of France, John Dee was astrologer to Queen Elizabeth I. Calisthenis, an astronomer, who spread this science in East was instructed by the Alexander the Great to accompany him to his country to spread this science there.

In India, Sage Parasar is regarded as the founder of astrology and spread this science through his disciples, Parasar is father of Vyas who wrote Geeta, Mahabharat and Vedas and other religious books. He had a laboratory and provided a "television" to Sanjay, the sarthi (one who drives the chariot of the King) who saw every thing through a television like view and narrated everything to King Dhristrastra

Below are listed some luminaries in the world of Astrology.

Arya Bhat

He was born in 476 AD. He belonged to Patliputra. Arya Bhatiyam is an astronomical work written by Arya Bhat. He was the earliest to give us the correct value of Pye to four decimal places. Matters relating to the Rule of 3, Trigonometrical expositions etc. are some of the fields of mathematics handled by him.

Varah Mihira

He was born in a village called Akapittaka in Ujjain (Avantika) in 505 AD. He was the son of a Brahmin named Aditya Das. His name was Mihir. Varah was the title given to him by King Vikramaditya. He died in 587 AD. He has written the following Books.

1. Brihat Jataka

2. Brihat Samhita

3. Pancha Siddhantika

4. Yoga Yatra

5. Laghu Jataka

6. Vivaha Patalam

7. Prasna Mahodedhi

8. Prasna Chandrika

9. Daivagnya Vallavh.

Kalyan Verma

He was born in 578 AD. He belonged to Rewa (Gujarat) He was written the book Saravali in which he admits that he is just reflecting the views of those ancient writers Atri, Prasar, Garga etc. He says that the Creator has written the future of man on his forehead and one can read it through the eyes of Jyotish.

Brahama Gupta

He hailed from Saurashtra. He was born in 598 AD. He was the son of Jishnu. He was the author of two good astronomical works, one Brahmas Pahupa Siddhanta and another Khanda Kadyaka, Brahma Gupta refuted the theory of Precession of Vishnu Chandra, author of Vashisht Siddhanta and attributes the cause of change in season to the motion of Sun only, and not to precessional motion of the Equinoxes.

Sridharacharya

Sridharacharya also known as Bhatta Sridhar, was a great mathematician. He was born in 951 AD in the village Bhuskrishti situated in the Distt. of Radha in Bengal. His father's name was Baldev Sharma.

He had written two distinguished works on mathematics, Patti Ganita and an abridged version of the work known as Trisatika. Trisatika is just the essence of Patti Ganita. He has dealt with Sunya Tatwa, the mathematics of zero in a distinctive manner. He has also dealt with the Rule of three, square, square root, cube and cube root, mixture, heaps of grain, shadow measurement and plane figures etc.

Sripathi

This celebrated author and eminent scholar was born in 999 AD in Berar (Maharashtra). He was the son of a Brahmin named as Nagdev. He has written the following books :

1. *Dheekoti Karna* which was written in 1039 AD. It is a short treatise on astronomy dealing with an easy way to compute the solar and lunar eclipses.

2. *Jyotish Ratna-Mala* which was written in 1040 AD.

3.   *Jataka Paddhati* popularly knows as Sripathi Paddhati deals with predictive astrology and pays proper attentions to Shadbala.

4.   *Siddhanta Shekar* deals with astronomy and algebrical operations discussions on spheres, astronomical instruments etc.

5.   *Dhurava Manasa Karna* was written in 1056 AD and deals with astronomy

6.   *Daivagnya Vallabh* is a work on Hora Muhutra and contains Panchanga details.

7.   *Ganita Tilak* deals with mathematics. It is known Patti Ganita.

8.   *Beeja Ganita* is a treatise on algebraic operations.

CHAPTER 3

Psychology vs. Astrology

According to both Laymen and Scholar, psychology literally means a science of mind or soul. It is composed of two words psyche and logos. Psyche means mind and logos means seasoned discourse or science.

Psychology may be defined as the science of human and animals behaviour. Behaviour includes all activities of an organism which can be observed by another person or by means of an experimenter's instruments. All behaviour cannot be observed by our senses, some can be better observed by utilising certain techniques. A number of internal process like thinking, eating etc. are regarded as behaviours of an organism. Many of these cannot be observed directly but something about them can be inferred from the hehaviour of an organisn. Because of its close relation with biological science, it is not only interested in human behaviour but also in animal behavour.

Study of behaviour of lower animals is very useful in understanding human beings because of great similarities in human and animal behaviour. There are many branches of psychology as given below :

1.   Clinical Psychology.

2.   Counselling Psychology

3.   Experimental Psychology.

4.   Industrial Psychology.

5.   Educational Psychology

6.   Schcool Psychology

7.   Social Psychology.

8.   Developmental Psychology

1. Clinical Psychology

Clinical psychology is that branch of psychology in which a psychology deals with abnormal behaviour of a person. Abnormal behaviour is that behaviour which is not according to social norms and not accepted by society and its culture. A clinical psychology is well trained in actionlogy of various form of abnormal behaviour such as psycho-neurosis. psychosis, mental retardation and any other forms of abnormal behaviour. The literal meaning of abnormal is being away from normal.

2. Counselling Psychology

In this branch the psychology, the psychologist deals with certain human problems. We always encounter a number of problems of school and college students. The person who deals with human problems is known as a psychological counseller. It must be admitted that the counsellors are custodians of the meantal health of the peoples for they are often reponsible for saving a lot of trouble, difficulties and unhappiness.

3. Experimental Psychology

It is one of the fundamental subfields of psychology. Fundamental in the sense that it carries on research and experimental work of many basic aspects of behaviour.

4. Industrial Psychology

The application of psychology in industrial and business fields. started with the use of psychology tests for the selection of the right workers for the right job but currently its scope has broadened so much that it already has its two separate subdivisions known as Personnel psychology and Engineering psychology.

5. Education Psychology

Educational psychology and school counselling are two interrelated sub-fields of psychology but their objective and aims are not same. Educational psychologists are more concerned with general psychological principles underlying the entire process of education. The main questions which an educational psychologist tries of answer are: When to teach? What to teach? and How to teach? Educational psychology tries to answer questions in the light of studies based on the development of the psychological process in human beings.

6. School Psychology

The school psychologists are more concerned with the problems of individual students than with the general principles of education. Their main task is to help students with various problems in adjusting to the school or college situation.

7. Social Psychology

Social psychology is that branch of psychology which deals with the social norms rules and regulation and inter-relationship between human beings. It is mainly concerned with the influence of various social worlds, it is concerned with the behaviour of man as a member of a social group.

8. Development Psychology

The main objective of development psychology is to investigate the changes in human behaviour that accompany changes with age. The individual's growth in his environment and culture forms its major concern so that he know himself better as well as those around him. Child psychology is only a part of developmental psychology though an important part, children grow rapidly and early influences on behaviour leave their lasting marks on human personality.

Astrology

Astrology is a divine science. It is the science of the influence of the stars on human beings Astrology is derived from the word "Aster" which means star and logos which means logic or reason.

An Astrologer gives mental strength to the feeble and weak minded, solace to the depressed, peace to anxious and worried to those who are of wavering mind. Varahmihir has said, that the astrologer should pay proper attention of the position of the Moon of his client. Moon foretells the temperament of his client. An astrology words should be so expressed that they do not hurt his client.

Clinical

During a psycho-analysis session a patient is seated amidst comfortable surroundings. He is then encouraged to narrate all his experience especially childhood ones. He is also administered small doses of tranquilizers. A psycho analysis censors the experience and detects the causes of tension. In a lot of cases a close examination however reveals that a major portion of the patient's fears are imaginary.

An astrology knows that when the Moon is associated with a node, and it is devoid of the benefic aspect of Jupiter, which can neutralize the evil effects of the conjunction of the native. In its absence, trust fails and suspicion rules. Trust and suspicion must be properly balanced in life otherwise a person's agony cannot be described in words.

An astrologer provides relief to the person by discussing all props and cons when the patient asks "How will he recover, when he had already consulted prominent doctors". The astrologer pin points the period of beginning of the misery and tells the end also. The client then tallies the past and feels satisfied that his good days are ahead. An astrologer also gives sermons to his client and guides him through the various storms that lash his life.

Counselling

The astrologer is also a good lawyer. His advise is alwyas welcomed. A person came to an astrologer and said "My wife has again cheated me, I want to go her house to beat her and the family members. The astrologer screened the chart and said."You are running a very bad period. Do not precipitate matters. The combination provides a clue that you may be behind the bars". The client said "I am well known to so many high ups. Nothing will happen". The astrologer replied "They may entangle you in Dowry Act and it may be difficult for you to free yourself". Once a good looking man came to the astrologer and said "I do not know why I am not getting married though I am over 30 years. Why God is so unkind to me?" The astrologer reviewed the chart and said "You are destined to marry after a year." The querent was satisfied.

It is our experience that when troubles come, they come like an army and counselling by an astrologer provides solace to the native.

Experimental

Original asrologers like sage-Parasar, Jamini and others have experimented so much that if we lay our on old classics. there is no room for experimentation there.

They studied the effects of Various planets of human affairs and then the rules were framed. *But in order to keep pace with the changiing society classical texts have to be updated.*

Industrial

Irrespective of the fact that a person is serving as a General Manager or a Production Manager one must have the qualities of leadership i.e. fine thinking and ability to take decisions and carry them through in spite of various constraints. Men are different in nature, temperament etc. No two persons are alike. A careful examination of the individual chart can reveal comprehensive picture of his psychological set up.

An astrologer can help the management by screening the horoscopes of the persons and his advise will prove an asset for the management.

To sum up a good astrologer helps in dispelling fears from the mind of the querist and prepares him/her to face the future with confidence and hope. He helps a person to have a glimpse of the unknown future. Prior knowledge helps the enquirer to reconcile himself to the situation.

In Ramayan when Sita asks the role of an astrologer, sage Valmiki replies, "Astrologer provides a ray of hope to his client by getting that the good period will start from such and such date.

CHAPTER **4**

Planets in the Sky and their
different conditions

PLANETS IN THE SKY

Sun in the Sky

Sun is the centre of all lives force and energy, According to the Hindu mythology the chariot of Sun is driven by seven horses.

Fig. 1. Sun with Seven Horses

Sun is positive and hot by nature, it rules the east direction, offers the power of resistance and is fiery by nature.

IT SIGNIFIES:

GENERAL   :   King, father, captain, command, boldness, brilliance, health, happiness, hope, political power, personality, dignity, soul, elevation, ambition, fame and east direction.

PARTS OF THE
BODY   :   Heart, head, brain. bone, right, eye mouth, spleen, throat, lungs, eye.

DISEASES   :   Heart trouble, headache, weak eye sight, baldness, low blood pressure, sun stroke, high fever.

PRODUCTS   :   Gold, copper, ruby.

FOOD STUFFS: Wheat, gur, orange, coconut, chillies, medicinal herbs.

ANIMALS   :   Lion, horse.

Astronomy

According to Hindu mythology, the chariot of Sun is driven by seven horses. Let us link it with Newton's dispersion of Sunlight Issac Newton knew astrology.

Newton's basic experiment with a prism allowed a narrow beam of sunlight to pass through a small hole in the window shutter. He noticed that white, on passing through the prism, spread out in the rainbow coloured strip which he could receive on a screen.

This coloured band is called the Spectrum and the phenomenon of the incident ray (which is the white light) breaking up into its constituent colours is called dispersion. A prism is thus said to disperse or analyse white sunlight into its various colour components, mainly a band of seven colours : Red, Orange, Yellow, Green, Blue, Indigo and Violet (Figure 2). This is called a visible specturm because,

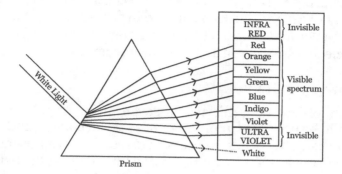

Fig. 2. *Diagram to show the visible and invisible parts of an extended solar specturm (sun's specturm).*

our eyes can see it. All the colours of the visible spectrum have different wave lengths, with red colour having the longest weblength, and violet colour having the shortest wavelength. The formation of spectrum consisting of seven colours shows that the visible part of sunlight comprises of seven different colours.

Wave Length

In many respects light has wave properties. The distance from crest to crest in light waves-as in water waves is called a wave-length.

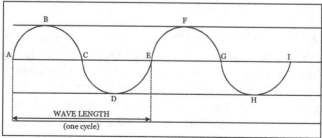

Fig. 3. *Wavelength*

Frequency

The number of crests which pass a fixed point in a given time (say one second) is the frequency of the wave and can be measured in crests or cycles per second (CPS). Tracing a link between the Sun Chariot used in the Hindu mythology and Newton's Prism". The readers may themselves decide the closeness between astrology and science.

Synthesis of Light

If white light be a mixture of seven different colours, it should be possible to combine these seven colours and get white light. Newton's experiment to test this is represented in Fig. 4 below a narrow beam of white light is allowed to fall on one face of prism. P1, so that the usual specturm is obtained in the emergent light. The rays emerging from P1 are than allowed to fall another exactly similar prism P2 which is so arranged as to refract the light in the opposite direction with respect to the first.

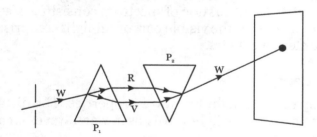

Fig. 4. *Synthesis of Light*

The light emerging from the second prism is received on a screen. The patch of light on the screen does not show any colour so we can presume it is white. Obviously, the dispersion of the rays of different colours, produced by the first prism, is cancelled by the equal and opposite dispersion produced by the second prism. In this experiment the prism P1 breaks the white light *(that is analyses it)* into its component colours; then the prism P2 collects these broken components and remix them in their correct proportion (that is synthesize them), so as to give back the light of the original white colour.

It is to be noted that the combination of the two prisms P1 and P2 above, is in fact equivalent to a rectangular slab glass with parallel sides. We know that when light passes through such a slab, the emergent ray is parallel; to the incident ray and there is on dispersion into colour.

Tracing the Link : Sun rules over the visible and the invisible spectrum. All the rays emanate from it. In other words all the 9 rays combined together are the Sun's rays. THAT IS WHY SUN IS CONSIDERED AS THE KING AND HOW THE OTHER PLANETS ARE ASSIGNED CABINET RANK WILL BE DISCUSSED ONE BY ONE. BY VIRTUE OF ITS POSITION AS THE KING, IT IS BOLD, COMMANDING, HAS POLITICAL POWER, DIGINITY. NAME AND FAME. LION IS THE KING OF ANIMALS AND SUN REPRESENTS LION. SINCE HORSE IS THE 'VAHANA' OF THE KING IT HAS BEEN INCLUDED SUN RISES IN THE EAST AND INDICATES EAST DIRECTION. IT IS HOT BY NATURE.

Astrologer do not restrict their observations at visible wave length, where the eye is sensitive. Many other wave lengths exist, undetected by the unaided eyes. Every object at any temperature above absolute zero (-273 detrees C) radiates at all the wave lengths of the electromagnetic spectrum. Scientists detect the composition of substances by studying the wave length of light they emit when hot. It is observed that elements emit light of a definite colour which has a definite wave length. By studying the wave length of light emitted by the Sun, it can be concluded that Sun is largely made up of Hydrogen.

A group of Alchemists, for fear that others may not make use of their knowledge and experience, adopted symbols instead of a product. The symbol used for Hydrogen is O. In astrology it represents Sun.

Sun represents bones, eyes, heart, head, brain. mouth, spleen, throat and lungs in the body. Let us discuss the source of vitamin D and how it helps the body. In subsequent chapters the author, taking the aid of astrophysics, chemistry and physiology shall presents articles in such a way that even those who know very little about science will be able to understand.

Astro Physicist

Ultra violet rays : Palm, in 1890, drew attention to the relationship between lack of exposure to sunlight and the incidents of rickets. It is well known, too, that rickets tend to appear after the dark winter months to be healed during the bright summer months.

These problems are seen especially in people not exposed to sun light like women in purdah and children staying in dark houses. The practice of exposing newborns to sunlight daily and oil massage is a preventive measures against these problems.

There are two source of Vitamin D for human being, the photo conversion of skin sterols and the diet. Our skin contains large amounts of a compound called 7-dehydrocholesterol. When ultra violet rays fall on our skin then this compound is converted into Vitamin D. Its chemical name is calciferol or Vitamin D_2. The compound 7 – dehydrocholesterol already presents in the skin is first converted to cholecalciferol or Vitamin D_3 in addition to sterols sources in the skin Vitamin D_3 can be derived from dietary sources. It is normally found in egg yolk, butter. fish and liver oil. Vitamin D2 (calciferol) is formed by ultra-violet irradiation of ergosterol, a substance found only in lower plants such as yeast and fungi.

Calcium and phosphate are two minerals which are necessary for the formation of healthy teeth and bones. Deficiency of calcium or phosphorus leads to malformation of bones and teeth. It is important to note that the absorption of calcium and phosphorus in our body takes place only in the presence of Vitamin D. Even if there is sufficient calcium and phosphorus in the diet but with the deficiency of Vitamin D, malformation of bones and teeth can take place.

Tracing Link

That is why the Sun in astrology represents bones. As every thing shines on account of sunlight - Sun represents eyes in astrology. The king is the head of the State and also the Sun in astrology represents head and brains. Sun is the centre of all lives. force and energy, and if offers the power of resistance and is a planet for vitality.

Absorption of Vitamin D, in the Small Intestines

It is available in foods of animal origin like milk. butter, egg yolk, fish liver oil and certain plant sources like yeast and grams have smaller quantity of an inferior quality of Vitamin D_2 which is not of much importance.

The yield from both the sources that is photo conversion and dietary is the inactive form the Vitamin D_3. This is activated in two steps each of adding hydroxyl (OH) group, first in the liver then in kidney. This forms dihydroxy Vitamin D_3 which is in an active form. It acts at various levels.

1.   Intestine mucosa-To stimulate absorption of calcium phosphate and its own inactive form, the absorbed minerals are transported to the blood, where the levels are maintained stringently. Calcium is used for bone mineralisation, nerve stimulation and muscles (heart and others) contraction by medicated eletro chemical changes. Excess is lost through urine.

2.   KIDNEY : Helping in reabsorption of filtered calcium and regulating the amount of its active form produced by stimulating hydroxylation when

levels of dihydroxy D_3 are low and inhibiting when high.

Tracing Link

From the above it is clear that Sun represents intestines etc. and also represents the diseases caused to these parts of the body.

Moon in the Sky

Moon is the queen of the planetary system. It takes 27 days, 7 hours and 43 minutes in transacting 12 signs. It is nearest to the earth and revolves around it. It shines by the reflected rays of the Sun. Moon governs the menstrual cycles of the ladies which also occurs for around 27 days. Moon is a cold planet. It waxes and wanes.

IT SIGNIFIES:

GENERAL : Mother, mind, water, milk, mental peace, public life, holding high position, impregnation, conception, birth of a child, infant stage, North West direction.

PARTS OF THE BODY: Blood, stomach, breast of the ladies.

DISEASES : Cold, cough, throat trouble, dysentry, vomitting, hydrocele, lunacy, hysteria, epilepsy, weak memory, depression, fear and inferiority complex.

FOOD STUFFS : Oranges, melon, cucumbers, palm, sugarcane, fruit juice, milk, curd, cream, butter, ghee betel leaves, acquatics, cooked food, salt, rice.

PRODUCTS : Pearl, silver

ANIMALS : Cow

Physiography

In physiography we read that tides in the sea are caused by the difference of attraction exerted by Moon and the centre of the Earth on the surface of water. The Moon attracts the sea water to itself causing tides and Sun hinders the action of Moon in lowering the tides.

Tides are caused by the gravitational pulls of the Sun and the Moon. The Sun's influence on the tides is less than half that of the Moon, because the Sun is too far away. All the same, the Sun countervails and supports the Moon's pull. Alternately, when the Sun, the Moon and Earth are in a line as at new and full moon, the Sun and the Moon combine their powers and we have very high tides called *spring tides*. When the Sun and the Moon are at right angles, as in the Moon's first and third quarters, the Sun acts as a counter balancing force and reduces the Moon's pull. During these periods. we experience very low tides called *neap tides*.

Composition of sea water is a mixture of various salts. The salts present in the sea are mainly of sodium, magnesium, calcium and potassium, Sea water contains about 3.6 percent by mass of dissolved salts which include the following :

	Mass %	*Relative %*
Sodium Chloride	2.8%	77.9%
Magnesium salts	0.6%	16.8%
Calcium salts	0.1%	2.7
Potassium salts	0.1%	2.7

The ocean covers 71% of the earth's surface. The volume of blood in our body is about 5 litres. It is composed of plasma and cell. The plasma or fluid portion of blood consists of 91% water and 9% solid products like proteins, salts, products of digestion and waste products. Normally blood is red when the oxygen is high and bluish when it is low. If we analyse the composition of blood, it is observed that blood contains nearly 80% sodium. 4% calcium and 4% potassium.

Drawing comparisons-if we take the percentage of different salts in sea water, it contains 77.9% sodium chloride as against 80% sodium in human blood. Similarly calcium and potassium are 2.7% each in sea water as against 4% each in human blood. Sea water and human blood thus have similar proportions. Both are affected by the gravitational pull of the Moon. Ordinary water is not attracted by Moon as it does not contain these salts, that is why pull on a river is not visible as is observed in sea water. Moon represents the mind because human blood is also attracted by the gravitational pull of Moon and blood practically conforms the same proportion of salts as does sea water. Moon represents water, milk, mind, mental peace, impregnation and conception. The role of Moon is predominant as the formation of an egg in females is on account of menses caused by the Moon.

There are 27 constellations in the Zodiac and Moon transits these 27 constellations within a period of 27 days and a few hours. Impregnation and conception is directly ruled by Moon. As there is a change in the behaviour of a person because blood which contains different salts, is attracted by the pull of the Moon and that is why it is said that Moon represents mental peace. The word Lunar means one who has faith in luna (Moon) and from Luna the word lunatic is formed. This means luna (Moon) has direct effect on a lunatic. If one happens to visit Asylum during full Moon days, a mad person will be very hostile the wild sea water that is why it is said in astrology that "Chandrama Manso Jayate" i.e., Moon signifies the mind.

Biological disorders of the body and mind are deeply connected with astrology. The missing links are now slowly falling into place.

Moon includes the breast of the lady as well as the milk which flows from the breast to feed the newborn, Cow gives us milk which is a sustainer and cow has been included under Moon.

The rays of Moon are cold by nature and in astrology it has been stated that a weak Moon causes cold, cough, throat trouble (which is as a result of cold) dysentery, vomiting (diseases of water). It also includes lunacy. hysteria, epilepsy and all have a direct relation with the mind. Weak Moon also is responsible for a weak memory, depression, fear and inferiority complex. It includes aquatic animals because they are available in water, salt pearl are available in water. Rice had been included as a product of the Moon as at the time of harvesting much water is needing for rice and similarly at the time of cooking, rice is soaked in water before cooking.

A few persons have done experiments on the aspect; Dr. K. Kalisko experimented and proved that maximum growth of wheat corresponded with the period of increasing Moon and just after the Summer Solstice and that Maize was found to grow best when planted two days day before full moon.

Our failures in the garden can be turned into successes when we follow the phases of the Moon and discover the best times of plating for abundant harvests. There is no doubt that some people have green fingers, everything they plant seems to flourish. They choose the correct phases of the Moon and for best results, plant when the Moon is in a sign favourable for sowing and planting.

Dr. Arnold Leiber found significant correlations between violent acts like murder, assault etc. with the waxing and waning Moon. The danger period according to his research, is when the Moon is full or when it is new Moon, (the period when the Sun, the Moon and earth lie in straight like). He examined 2000 cases from 1956 to 1970 and his results, he admits are displeasing to the rational scientific outlook.

Venus in the Sky

Venus is the goddess of love. When cupid strikes, emotions govern and rationality takes a back seat. Venus governs passion, artistic beauty, electronic items, material comforts, sensual pleasures. It signifies a pleasing personality, calmness, patience, grace and soft spokenness. Being a chief governor for carriage, it can make or mar it. It represents:

GENERAL	:	Love affairs, pleasure of spouse, family bliss, beautiful clothes, eye luster, dens of prostitutes, passion, meat intoxicating drinks, south-east direction and peace.
PARTS OF THE BODY	:	Chin, cheeks, throat, eyes, reproductive system, kidney, curly hair.
DISEASES	:	Venereal disease, gonorrhea, syphilis, complaints due to over sex, skin disease, eczema, leprosy and leucoderma. It also rules over infection in the eyes.
PRODUCTS	:	Silk and rayon, hosiery (ladies), embroidery, tailoring, machine, perfumery, fancy goods photographs, cotton silver, copper, glass, rubber, plastics petrol, cars, ships and aeroplanes.
FOOD STUFFS	:	Sugar, confectionary, milk, coffee, tea, flowers, figs, cherries, apples, juicy and tasty fruits.

Venus in Chemistry

In the combined state, carbon occurs in the forms of :

  (i)   Carbonates (limestone, marble, dolomite)

  (ii) Petroleum and natural gas

(iii) Proteins and fats

(iv) Carbon dioxide (in the air)

Pure carbon occurs in the form of diamond and graphite. Diamonds are formed from the carbon present in the upper mantle at a depth of over 150 km. in the earth, under conditions of high temperature and high pressure. Diamond is the hardest natural substance known. When diamond is burnt in pure oxygen, carbon dioxide is formed and nothing is left behind. On account of its extra ordinary brilliance, which is due to its great ability to reflect light, diamonds are used for making jewellery, Because of its ability to keep out harmful radiations, diamonds are used by eye-surgeons as a tool to remove cataract from eyes with great precision.

The organic compounds obtained from planets are sugar, starch, cellulose, vegetable oils, essential oils, drugs, dyes and insecticides. Animal tissue gives us fats and oils.

Hydrocarbon

A compound made up of hydrogen and carbon is a hydrocarbon. The most important natural source of hydrocarbons is petroleum (crude oil). The natural gas which occurs above petroleum deposits also contains hydrocarbons, Natural Rubber contains unsaturated hydrocarbons.

Astronomy

Astronomers observed through the study of wave length that Venus contains dense carbon dioxide.

Biology

In Biology ♀ is a female symbol.

Alchemist

Alchemist symbol ♀ is of silver.

An alchemist who uses code language to indicate the product/mental uses the symbol ♀ to represent silver. Silver is a white metal which is used in silvering of mirrors and silver plating. Silver bromide used in photography. Photographic plate consists of a glass plate of celluloid which is coated with a thin layer if emulsion of silver bromide.

Tracing Link

Ladies have a fancy for silk and rayon, embroidery, perfumes etc. as these items are ruled by Venus. In biology the symbol ♀ is of female in astrology this symbol is of Venus who is depicted as a female. Tailoring machine is normally used by ladies. Silver has been included as the item of Venus on account of alchemist symbol. Silver is used in photography. Sugar contains 27% carbon. Similarly petrol also contains carbon. Petrol is widely used in cars, aeroplanes. etc. and LPG which is a form of carbon as discussed earlier has been included in Venus. Diamond is also carbon and cataract is removed with the help of diamond (carbon). As Venus is a feminine planet, chin, cheeks, throat, eyes, and curly hair attract the opposite sex and these have been included in Venus. Females have a pleasing personality, graceful manners refined nature and are soft spoken. So women have been attributed Venus like characteristics.

The ladies have a reproductive systems in the body. Sex diseases like veneral (from Venus) gonorrhea, syphilis, and diseases on account of over sex are ruled by Venus. Skin diseases spoil the beauty of the body. Eczema, leprosy and leucoderma etc. are ruled by Venus Retina is ruled by Venus and cataract is the disease of the eye.

So from various science and streams we observe that Venusian traits and a human's behaviour are linked. Quite naturally then when Venus rules over a person he seeks comforts, materials pleasures and Cupid, Planets have a tremendous influence on a human as well as his surroundings. Astrology thus is not an isolated science, it impinges on most aspects of life.

Jupiter in the Sky

Jupiter is considered to be a teacher and a preceptor who removes ignorance and darkness and provides wisdom to his disciple. Jupiter provides providential help at the appropriate time and helps to tide over the difficulties. As Jupiter is a preceptor, it represents social justice, religion, pilgrimage, sincerity, wisdom occult science, law truth and honesty. in olden days Physicians used to administer medicine in the Hora ruled by Jupiter.

GENERAL : Ordinary clothes, religion, educations, occult, science, prosperity, wealth, pilgrimage, morality, wisdom and astrology.

WHEN AFFLICTED : Liberal, extremist, extravagant, careless, over optimistic, gambling mis-judgement, poverty, unpopularity.

PARTS OF THE BODY: Liver tumours, circulation of blood arteries, facts in body, kidney, thigh, feet, right ear,

DISEASES : Liver complaints, jaundice, dropsy, flatulence, abscess, cerebral congestion, carbuncles, diabetes, vertigo, catarrh.

PRODUCTS : Gold, topaz, platinum, rubber

FOOD PRODUCTS : Orange, banana, peepal tree, yellow colour, flowers and vegetable, gram pulses, all sweet eatables

ANIMALS : Horse, elephant, ox etc.

Astronomy

Jupiter is a giant amongst the planets. If the mass (weight) of the earth is to be assumed as 1, the mass of the Jupiter in relation to earth is 317.89. Its mass is 71 percent of the total mass of the planetary systems. It has one and half times the volume of all other planets combined.

Its size is so big that thirteen earths can easily fit in it. As against the earth's density of 5.5, the density of Jupiter is 1.3 *i.e.* roughly one fourth of the earth's density.

It is made up of 89 percent hydrogen and 11 percent helium with smaller amounts of other substances like Hydro compounds including ammonia. water and ammoniun hydrosulphite. It is on account of this that the density of Jupiter is one fourth of the earth's. Methane and ammonia, which are formed when hydrogen combines with carbon and nitrogen respectively, are also present in the atmosphere of Jupiter.

Jupiter radiates 1.7 times more energy than it would do if it depended only upon radiation received from the Sun. All other planets draw from the Sun whatever energy they possess. Jupiter emits random bursts of intense radio energy at ion wave lengths. It is the most powerful radio object in the solar systems, next only to the Sun. No other planet is known to possess radio-energy of its own.

Fig. 5. *Jupiter with its Red Spot as seen by Voyager I from distance of over 30 million kilometers. (Courtesy : JPL/NASA).*

When all colours of the spectrum obtained by one prism were blocked off except one, say yellow, by using an opaque screen having a small hole in it and this light of single colour was made to pass throug another prism, it was observed that the yellow ray was bent out of its path by the prism (refraction) but did not change colour, that is yellow remained yellow. Newton repeated this experiment with each colour. The colours did not split any further, as the white light done. He noticed, however that each colour was deviated by a different amount as it passed through the second prism.

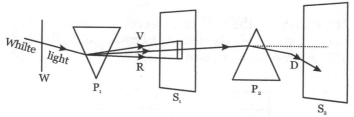

Fig. 6. *Colour passing through another prism by Newton*

In Chemistry, the alchemist used this symbol with (♃) which represents gold. In astrology this symbol (♃) is of Jupiter. If we take the mass (weight) of all the planets, the mass of Jupiter with relation to all the planets combined together is 71 percent. This mass of different planets is as under :

Jupiter	317.89
Saturn	95.17
Mars	0.55
Earth	1.00
Venus	0.815
Mercury	0.056
Uranus	15.00
Neptune	17.00
Pluto	0.9

(If the mass of the earth is assumed as I)

Guru in Sanskrit is one who has more weightage. It is on account of this quality (Mass) of Jupiter, that it is considered as a Guru. Guru is a person who knows much more than an ordinary person. Let us take the volume of the different planets.

JUPITER	1318.7
SATURN	744
MARS	0.56
VENUS	0.86
MERCURY	0.056

It we analyse the different secret symbols as used by Alchemist and if we take density of each metal, the density of different metals shall be as under:

Metal	Density
GOLD	19.3
MERCURY	13.6
LEAD	11.3
SILVER	10.5
COPPER	8.9
IRON	7.8

The alchemist symbol ♃ which is a secret symbol represents Gold. Gold has the maximum density and is the most precious amongst the metal. That is why Jupiter represents Gold.

Gurus in olden times used to live in the forest. They had a fascination for different types of planet and had a wide knowledge or medicinal plants available near their dwellings.

Before they prescribed any medicine they used to invoke the blessings of the Divine power. There was an invisible aura around them. Sometimes a patient could the cured just by coming into contact with this aura. Medicines were however given so that their accrued Bhakti power does not diminish. Speaking of present times, pious physicians even now a days can cure patients with the help of holistic methods of medicines such as regulated diet, strengthening of will power to survive and emotional support. Generally observing, physicians now a days put a symbol R_x on the prescription slip before prescribing any medicine. It resembles R_x a bar (I), before ♃ The symbol representing Jupiter overseas health and well being. Generally when we see the body of the preceptor in most of the cases their belly is much more than their chest and their weight is also more. It is also an Astronomical quality of Jupiter. That is why Jupiter in astrology represents liver and kidney. Taking more food and less exercise is responsible for liver disease and there will be excess fat in the body. This excess fat in the body will affect the circulation of blood and will cause lever complaints. jaundice, abscess, cerebral congestion, diabetes and thereby damage to kidney. Carbuncle is also an abscess in a particular part of the body. Jupiter is considered as a preceptor in astrology. It radiates 1.7 more energy than received from the Sun. When we go to a temple or a religious place we offer a little offering and in lieu of that we ask in plenty. Even when we go to a preceptor with offerings, in return by way of blessings, he gives us much more than we have offered to him.

The basic qualities of a preceptor are that he likes social justice, sincerity, truth, honesty and obedience, If we analyse the qualities of a preceptor we see that he removes ignorance and darkness and provides wisdom to his disciples.

In astrology the products included in Jupiter are gold, topaz , platinum and the products of yellow colours. The preceptors used to sit under a peepal tree as it provides maximum oxygen. They took sweet eatables and fruits and these are included as the qualities of Jupiter. They used ordinary clothes and horse, elephants, cows etc. kept in their place of living. Pulses made out of black gram are of yellow colour and all our preceptors used to wear yellow colour clothes. It is one of the properties of gold that it does not tarnish when exposed to air or oxygen even at high temperatures. Common acids do not attack it, if used singly. It is generally alloyed with copper. Guru (Jupiter) has the same quality and is not influenced by others.

The relations between science and astrology is ancient, linked in many places and very enriching, Our failure to interpret every day phenomenon does not mean that events occur in isolation. Nature follows its own pattern. It is upto us to interpret it.

Mars in the Sky

Mars in the Commander-in-Chief of the planetary cabinet. It signifies fighting prowess and is a fiery and masculine planet. It symbolises energy both constructive and destructive. Martians will select opportune time to strike and also to withdraw. They inflict the worst type of injuries but when they want to help someone they help them at all costs.

IT SIGNIFIES:

GENERAL   :   Energy strength, vitality, practical, nature, obstinacy, landed property, accident, operation, wounds, cuts, bleeding, earthquake, military operations and south direction.

PARTS OF THE BODY :   Ear, nose, forehead, sinew, fibre, muscular tissues, gall bladder, prostate glands, uterus, external sex organs, rectum, testicles and red bone marrow.

DISEASES   :   Fever, small pox, chicken pox, measles, burns, wounds, tumours, eruptions, high blood pressure,

ENT diseases, bleeding, hernia, fistula, carbuncle, brain fever.

PRODUCTS   :   Iron and steel, red colour products, red coral, sulphur.

FOOD STUFFS   :   Ginger, garlic coriander, thorny plants, cashewnut, walnut groundnut, betel nut, coffee, gur.

ANIMALS   :   Tigers, hunting dogs and wolves.

The professions ruled by it are fireman, armament factories, solders, police, surgeons, dentist, barber, carpenter, butcher, cooks, boxers, chemists, druggists and military operations.

Tracing Links

In astrology this symbol ♂ represents Mars. In chemistry it denotes tin. It also indicates a spear which was used by primitive men as a mode of self defence and also to hunt animals & birds. In course of time, kings used spears as an instrument of warfare for their armies. Mars rules wars too. On the other hand ♂ symbol means tin which is a shining white metal.

It is used in tinning of utensils. It provides a protective coating around iron called tin plating. Barber's blade, Surgeon's knives etc. are all tin plated to provide the protective coating.

Thorny planets are a source of wounds on the human body and they have been included in Mars in astrology. Amongst hunting animals like tigers, hunting dogs, wolves have been included in Mars as they inflict injuries on other animals.

It has been stated that Mars who symbolise senses, rules over the animal instinct in men. It signifies energy both constructive and destructive. As a result of diseases there is likelihood of operation. In case of accidents or fight there are wounds, cuts, bleeding etc. The planet Mars in astrology is related to such operations. It also includes military operations. In fact the professions ruled by Mars are of soldiers or police who protect the Nation or the State. Similarly a barber uses a blade, carpenter uses a saw, butcher uses a knife and boxer uses force. The surgeon uses knives, scissors and allied instruments at the time of operation. If we analysis the behaviour of army we find that they are disciplined and they have to exercise daily in order to maintain health and Mars in astrology signifies energy, strength vitality and practical nature. Soldiers inflict worst type of injuries on their enemies. They also strike and withdraw according to the prevailing conditions. In case of war they try to protect the country and in case of natural calamities like earthquake, floods etc. they help the mankind.

Mars is a fiery planet and when gets burnt there are boils on the body as a results of burning. Mars rules over boil type disease small pox, chicken pox, measles etc. are the boil-type diseases which are visible on the body. Tumour is inflammatory and is however inside the body and is also ruled by Mars, The colour of blood is red, Mars rules over fever (increase in body temperature) burns, wound, bleeding hernia and fistula. On account of lack of vitality a person suffers from deformity and Mars rules over the deformation of body.

According to Newton's theory, Mars has the maximum wave length. Let us see the Newton's System of prism.

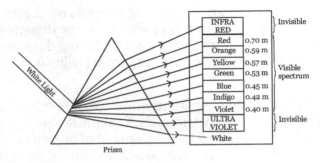

Fig. 7. *Diagram to show the visible and invisible parts of an extended solar spectrum (Sun's spectrum)*

This diagram lists the wave length of different colour, where 'M' stands for Micron, which is equaivalent to one part of a million. Mars has the maximum wave length. It means that within a short span Mars tries to cover more distance. To cover more distance in a lesser period, it is necessary that a person will have to drive rashly and thereby increasing chances of accidents. Mars is a planet of accidents. As a results of an accident, there may be cuts, wounds bleeding etc.

Red colour has the maximum wave length. On account of the maximum wavelength of Mars, nature has given the colour of blood as red so that it may immediately catch the eye. On account of the red colour of Mars, red coloured products like red coral, shellac, blood etc. are ruled by Mars.

An examination of white light specturm will show that one colour in it shades into the next without leaving any gap in between. This is because white light is composed of a very large number of colours, each of which is bent to a different extent depending on its wavelength. If the wavelength is longer, the ray bends less. Thus the long waves of red colour are bent the least that is why Mars in astrology is considered as obstinate, stubborn and eccentric. Military persons etc. do not bend (surrender) so easily on account of the inherent quality of Mars.

MARS IS CONSIDERED AS COMMANDER-IN-CHIEF NOT ONLY ON ACCOUNT OF ITS MAXIMUM WAVELENGTH BUT ALSO RED COLOUR IS ON THE TOP OF THE VISIBLE SPECTRUM signifying that a Commander is always on the top. In a competition those who run the fastest, get the medal.

Mars in Biology

Let us see what the ♂ implies in biology. The symbol ♂ represents a male. Mars is considered as a male in astrology on account of this symbol.

Mars is considered powerful during the night. All the attacks are normally made at night

Sulphur is used for fire arms etc. and has been included as a product ruled by Mars. Ginger, garlic, coriander, cashew nut, walnut, groundnut and betelnut provide heat to the body and that is why these have been included. Coffee, tea, tobacco and mid intoxicants are also ruled by Mars.

Mercury in the Sky

Mercury is considered as the prince of the planetary cabinet. The maximum distance between the Sun and Mercury can be 28 degrees. It is the prince and thereby a child. So. like a child, it will not independently and will follow the characteristics of the planet with whom it has an association.

It is a planet of oration and speech and on account of its fluent expression it produces good salesman. insurance agents and publicity agents who have to travel frequently. It is a planet of astrologers, astronomers, engineers and mathematicians. It also represents intellect, retentive memory and North direction.

IT SIGNIGFIES:

GENERAL	: Intelligence, quick grasp, retentive memory, logician, imagination, fluent expression, research, north direction, cleverness mischieviousness, lie.
PART OF THE BODY:	Solar plexus, central nervous system, tongue, abdomen, lungs, skin, arms.
DISEASES	: Mental weakness, nervous breakdown, impotency, deafness, stammering etc.
FOOD PRODUCTS :	Betal leaves, nuts, spinach, green

vegetables & pulses.

MINERALS   :   Emerald, limestone.

OTHERS   :   Green colour clothes, goat.

Astro Physicist

The alchemist used the code ☿ which represents Mercury, a metal. This symbol ☿ represents Mercury in astrology. Let us see the qualities of Mercury.

1.   It does stick to glass

2.   It can easily be obtained in pure form

3.   Its expansion is uniform

4.   It is a good conductor of heat.

Leaves (and stems sometimes) are green because they contain cell bodies called chloroplasts. This green coloured material (pigment) is called chlorophyll. Green plants used chlorophyll to trap energy from Sun light. They synthesise an organic compound called carbohydrate: using carbon dioxide and water from the environment and energy from Mercury light. Oxygen is thus released in the process.

Photo Synthesis

The terms "photo synthesis" means "building up by light". Photo-synthesis is the process by which green plants combine the carbon dioxide and water in the presence of Sun light to form food (glucose) and release oxygen. The process of photosynthesis is as under :

$$6 CO_2 + 6H_2O + \text{Light energy} \xrightarrow{\text{Photosynthesis}} C_6H_{12}O_6 + 6O_2$$

Carbon   Water   Glucose Oxygen

Dioxide

(From air) (From soil) (From Sun) (Chlorophyll) (A food)

Where CO_2 stands for Carbon Dioxide H_2O for water, $C_6H_{12}O_6$ for glucose and O_2 for oxygen.

Carbon dioxide used in photosynthesis comes from air and water comes from soil. It should be noted that photosynthesis takes place in the presence of a catalyst called chlorophyll, which is present in the plant leaf. The main point to be noted here is that energy (in the form of Sun light) is absorbed in the process of photosynthesis. The energy gets stored in the food in the form of chemical energy, which is released from our body during respiration.

Respiration

Respiration is the process by which living things breakdown food (glucose) by burning with the oxygen breathed in the form of air, to form carbon dioxide and water and to obtain energy required for living. The process of respiration can be represented as :

$$C_6H_{12}O_6 \ + \ 6O_2 \ \xrightarrow{\text{Respiration}} \ 6CO_2 \ + \ 6H_2O \ + \ \text{Heat}$$

Glucose   Oxygen   Carbon Dioxide   Water   Energy

(A Food) (from breathing air)

This reaction is opposite to that which takes place during photosynthesis. Thus photosynthesis is the formation of food by absorbing energy whereas respiration is the decomposition of food with the release of energy.

Thus photosynthesis produces food and respiration breaks down (oxidises) food. In photosynthesis, energy of sunlight is stored in food in the form of glucose whereas in respiration, the energy stored in food in the form of glucose is released by oxidation.

When we eat food, big molecules of food are broken down into small molecules of glucose, during the process of digestion. Glucose thus formed is absorbed in the blood and taken by blood to the cell throughout our body. When we breathe in air, oxygen of the air is absorbed by the blood and carried to all the cells where glucose is waiting for it. During respiration, the glucose present in the cells gets oxidised slowly to form carbon dioxide and water. The carbon dioxide formed during respiration dissolves in blood travels to the lungs and is breathed out.

The waste products of metabolism, formed in the tissues, enter the blood stream and are brought by it to excretory organs (kidney, bowels, lungs and skin). It is through the thin wall of the capillaries, which consist only of endothelium, that the various inter-changes take place. The celiac ganglia are tough modular masses, connected to each other by fibres that encircle the celiac trunk, the whole being known as celiac plexus, or the solar plexus, because its branches radiate, like the rays of the Sun.

Missing Links

From the above it is clear that Mercury represents solar plexus and central nervous system, abdomen, tongue (as it helps in swallowing and produces enzymes) biles, muscular tissues and skin. (based on photosynthesis). Diseases ruled by it are diseases of the abdomen, tongue, lungs, biles, skin, vocal organs, stammering, asthma (breathing trouble) etc. On account its green pigment, green coloured material, green pulses, spinach, betel leaves and other green products have been included as the products of Mercury. It includes vocal organs, oration, speech, salesmanship, astrology etc. all entirely based on oration or speech. Mercury is the fastest planet and people ruled by it have to travel extensively.

The colour of Mars is red which is hot by nature and the colour of Saturn is bluish grey which is cold. Green colour is medium. The wave length of red is 0.7 microns and that of violet 0.4 microns. Green colour is 0.53 microns. It is a colour of prosperity. It is mid way, Doctors use green colour clothes at the time operation and green colour clothes are used by patients who are to be operated. After operation of an eye, green colour cloth is used to protect eye from sun rays or light. Red colour will make the surgeon(s) rash and violet colour will make them slow. Green colour is medium. it is neither fast nor slow. It is remarkable how links can be traced between the properties of a planet, its resulting influence on animal and plant life and thereby even influences the human psyche.

Saturn in the Sky

Saturn is called Yama. Its colour is black or blue. The duty of Yama is to pronounce judgement based on our past Karmas. Its speed is very slow and it is said to be lame. Saturn is the Chief Governor of longevity. Being the son of Sun it is diametrically opposed to it. Saturn and Sun are lords of Aquarius and Leo which are opposite to each other. Sun is exalted in Aries whereas Saturn gets debilitated and Saturn is exalted in Libra where Sun gets debilitated. Gem ruled by Saturn is Neelam. Lord Shiva who has the power of destruction is called Neelkantha.

IT SIGNIFIES:

GENERAL	:	Delay, deceit, denial disappointment, distrust, disharmony, dispute, difference of opinion, plodding, pessimism, prudence, lethargia, inferiority complex, west direction.
WHEN AFFLICTED	:	Drunkenness, gambling, whirlwinds, storms.
PART OF THE BODY	:	Teeth, feet, bones, knees, ribs, nails, hair.
DISEASES	:	Paralysis, insanity, limb injury, cancer, heart pain, rheumatism, consumption.
FOOD PRODUCTS	:	Potato, tapioea, black pulses, barley, rye, mustard oil, crude oil, wine.
ANIMALS	:	Crow, buffaloes.

Astronomy

As already indicated while discussing the various aspects of Sun that according to Hindu mythology there are 7 horses of Sun. Let us once again discuss the visible spectrum as displayed by Newton.

The chemical composition of distant stars can be determined from the light which they radiate to us and the interpolation provided by modern physics.

According to Newton's theory of prism the violet rays of visible spectrum are at the bottom. The frequency of violet rays is more but the wave length is short. The wave length of red colour which represents Mars is just double of violet colour and the frequency is less. So more the frequency, lesser is the wave length.

Newton examined the rays further and found "If the wave length is longer, the rays bend less, if the wave length is shorter, it bends more. Thus the short waves of violet colour are bent the most, while the long waves of the red colour bend the least. Violet is vigorously bent, while red resists bending.

Alchemist

Alchemist who used code language gave the symbol ♄ which represents lead. Let us discuss the chemical properties of lead. (pb, as its chemical name).

I.   Lead is soft, bluish-grey metal. It marks paper black

II.   Underground telephone cables are protected by lead covering.

III. It is used in storage batteries.

IV.   It dissolves in water and is poisonous.

V.   It is used for soldering the joints.

VI.   Most powerful radioactive substances are kept in lead containers.

VII. It is used in the manufacture of bullets.

VIII. It is used in preparation of lead tetraethyl which is an anti knocking additive in petrol.

IX. It is used in paints & varnishes.

The basic quality of lead is that it adds durability or prolongs life such as durability to the batteries, underground telephone cables and paints & varnishes. Enhancing the durability of a product adds to the longevity of that product. As such Saturn is a planet of longevity. On account of its slow nature it signifies patience, perseverance, laziness, lethargia. In our daily lite when any event takes up longer than neccessary duration; frustration results because we are interested in quick results. Saturn thus is considered a planet for delays.

Lead is slow poison. Saturn is a servant. As such whenever Saturn is allowed to play its part, it pollutes and administers poison to a person. In our daily life we see the master is murdered by the help of the servant either directly or indirectly. As lead (Saturn) has too much power of retention and the Sun, (which we have discussed represents heart) when influenced by Saturn, results in a paralytic attack to a person. Low blood pressure is also caused on account of influence of Saturn on Sun.

If we analyse the prismatic dispersion of light, the violet colour wave length is short *i.e.* though it moves faster (higher frequency) yet it covers less distance. This quality of Saturn is derived from violet colour. Every age has been the age of competition and Mars always competes as it will cover more distance on account of long wave length and will command whereas Saturn will remain backward. On account of this quality, Saturn is treated as a servant. If we analyse the behaviour of a servant, we find that a servant acts as if he is too busy but he will be whiling away time and there will be less production (more frequency less wave length). Red colour which represents Mars is at the top of the visible spectrum i.e. one who commands and violet is at the bottom representing the servant. Alternatively the commander will resist bending whereas the servant can be influenced easily like bending of the violet waves vigorously.

Saturn is a planet of obstruction. It rules over lead which obstructs the rays of radioactive material. Some of most powerful radioactive substances like uranium and radium are kept in lead containers. Lead is used for soldering the joints and it adds durability. Teeth, bones, Knees, ribs, nails etc. which can be joined after a fracture are ruled by Saturn. Amongst the vegetables potato and tapioca are cheap and available throughout the year and can be afforded by poor people. The motion of Saturn is very slow and to denote slowness, Saturn is depicted as lame. Crow and buffalo have been included on account of black colour. Lead is also bluish grey. It is regarded as Yama because the duty of Yama is to give punishment based on our past karmas. Similarly all the Judges wear black colour clothes and a lawyer who tries to protect us also puts on black colour garment. On account of the slow nature of Saturn, judges take sufficient time in deciding a case and abnormal delay leads to disappointment. Wool is removed from the body of the lamp by poor persons and the skin is also removed by poor persons, skin, wool etc, are ruled by Saturn.

At a casual glance though we have read about lead, Saturn, prism, potatoes etc. in various sciences, and also the properties associated with each but little more than a casual glance is required to trace links between sciences and astrology and its resultant effect on us.

Rahu in the Sky

Rahu is not substantial body which can be observed in some shape or mass like any other planet. According to Hindu mythology, Rahu and Ketu are two parts of the body. Indian Rishis (Saints) who were in fact, inventors, astronomers and researchers visualised the effects of these shadowy planets very minutely. Science in those days was much more advanced than the present science.

As time elapsed science continued to decay and no solid explanation could be given by the modern astrologer on account of lack of co-ordination between Science and astrology.

IT SIGNIFIES:

GENERAL	:	Love affairs, evil thoughts, outcaste, dual marriage, manipulation, slowness.
PARTY OF THE BODY	:	Buttocks.
DISEASES	:	Amputation of the body parts, epidemics cough, boils, gastric trouble, acute pain.
PRODUCTS	:	Radio aerial, south, west direction, iron, gomedh.
FOOD STUFFS	:	Radish coconut, wine, meat, egg, halwa, fried products.
ANIMALS	:	Serpents, mosquitoes bugs.
OTHERS	:	Inventors, astrologers, spies.

If we study Newton's basic experiment with the prism, we are aware that he allowed a narrow beam of sun light to pass through it. On passing through the prism he noticed that the beam broke into its seven constituents colours. This is called a visible spectrum.

The wave length of visible spectrum is as under:

	(in microns)
Red	0.70
Orange	0.59
Yellow	0.57
Green	0.53
Blue	0.45
Indigo	0.42
Violet	0.40

One part of a million is called micron.

There are also two types of rays which are invisible. Both have a deep effect on us. Infra-red rays (radiation) and Ultra-violet rays. If we go beyond violet rays. there are ultra violet rays which are not visible. Ultra violet rays have been further extended as :

Ultra Violet Rays

Near Violet	Far Ultra violet	Extreme Ultra violet
0.40 to 0.30 microns	0.30 to 0.20 microns	0.20 to 0.10 microns

X-rays	Y-Rays	Gamma Rays	Cosmic Rays
10^{-10} 10^{-8M}	10^{-15} 10^{-13M}	10^{-13} 10^{-10M}	10^{-7} 10^{-13M}

If we go deep, we will find that we had taken two shadowy planets in astrology on account of these rays. Infra red rays and ultra violet rays are included in astrology on account of these rays. Infra red rays and ultra violet rays are invisible. In fact Indian scientists visualised the effect of these rays. They cause earthquakes and bring sudden changes in the climatic conditions which have been dealt elaborately in the author's other book.

We get ultra violet rays (radiation) from the Sun. In fact all the ultra violet radiation emitted by sun does not reach us on the earth. Most of the ultra violet radiation is absorbed by the ozone layer etc. present in the atmosphere. X-Rays have a short wave length but they have a high penetrating power. The harmful effect of X-rays or X-radiation is that it damages human tissues when it is exposed to X-rays for longer periods. The radiologist (doctor doing X-ray) or other technicians who handle X-Ray machine fall in the high risk area of radiation.

When we visit a hospital, we find there are different department for X-rays or Gamma rays. The specification for X-ray room include at least nine inches thick concrete walls and 0.6 mm lead screens on airtight doors and windows to avoid the passage of radiation outside the room where the equipment installed people who work on these machines are also supposed to wear lead-rubber aprons, gloves and goggles to protect themselves from the harmful effects of exposure to radiation.

Lead is a poisonous material but it acts slowly. Similarly X-rays also have lasting effect on human body. The effect of the Ultra-Violet rays, X-rays and Gamma rays were visualised by our scientists and they treated these two types of rays *i.e.* infra-red and ultra violet-rays as Ketu and Rahu respectively. As lead is a poisonous substanc serpents, worms mosquitoes, bugs etc. have been included. The ultra violet rays are invisible. So the astrologer talks about the invisible which will become visible at a later stage. The inventor also invents a hidden thing. Spies also collect and supply he information secretly. Love affairs are initially hidden and partners do not believe in casteism as such Rahu has been treated as outcaste. As Rahu rays are much penetrating it shortens the life of the life partner and it represents dual marriage, lead (Saturn) is slow and ultra violet being below the violet is slower and that is why it represents slowness. Gas trouble, body pain is not visible but it is felt by the individual. Radio waves are also invisible.

The alchemist used this sumbol ♋ for Rahu. In astrology. Rahu is a manipulator and a diplomat. It is very difficult to know how a diplomat will react or respond.

It we go beyond the X-rays, we know that Gamma radiation affects us as under:

1.   Nuclear radiation (like gamma radiation) disrupts cell membranes.

2.   Can cause leukemia and cancer.

3.   Induce *warted* cell division.

4.   Damage genes and chromosomes.

5.   Destroy tissues, cells and blood corpuscles.

The persons handling gamma radiation machines in hospitals for the treatment of Cancer, fall under high risk category.

A thorough study of ultra violet rays revealed all these facts and ultra violet rays were found to be more poisonous than lead. Their role starts after the visible spectrum. Astrology links ultra violet rays to Rahu. There is also an ancient saying "Sanivat Rahu" which means Rahu acts like Saturn. Hence all the attributes of Saturn are shared by Rahu with the added features of being invisible. Thus Rahu affects humans continously under cover and in a more potent form. The term Sanivat Rahu is on account of this reason.

Ketu in the Sky

Ketu stands for religion, final emancipation and spiritual pride. The outward appearance is started to be a red and fierce look venomous tongue, smoke colour and lean disposition. It includes :

GENERAL : Quarrels, deception, back biting, vicious tendencies, assassinations, intrigue.

FOOD : Horse gram

PRODUCTS : Turquoise (Gem).

OTHERS : Philosophers, occultists, astrologers, eunuch, ascetics.

Let us once again take a clue of Ketu through Newton's system of prism:

Green House Effect

Sun light consisting of ultra violet rays, visible light and inftra-red falls on the top of the atmosphere, then first of all harmfull ultra violet radiation is absorbed by the ozone layer. The visible rays and infra-red rays then pass through the carbon dioxide layer and fall on the surface of the earth.

The infra-red rays which come from Sun are of short wave length and pass through the carbon dioxide layer easily. These rays warm the earth and the various objects on the earth. But since the earth's surface and the objects on it are less hot, they emit infra-red rays of long wave length. The trapping of infra red radiation reflected from the earth's surface by carbon dioxide layer in the atmosphere is called green house effect.

Infra-red Rays

Infra-red radiation has an important property. It can heat-up an object in its path. The heat that we feel from Sun light is due to the presence of infra-red rays in it. A hot electric iron also emits infra-red rays, we can feel the heat when we come close to it. However, it is not hot enough to emit visible light.

In 1800, Herchell was trying to find the temperature corresponding to the different parts of the solar spectrum. He found that the temperature shown by a delicate thermometer increased progressively towards the end and attained a maximum value at a little distance beyond this end. This proved that the solar spectrum was not confined to the visible light radiations only, but extended to invisible infra-red spectrum, which has remarkable heating properties. These radiation are called the heat rays.

Infra-red rays are used in long range photography. It is possible to take clear pictures of mountain scenes about 100 kilometers away using a filter which allows only infra-red rays into a camera loaded with special infra-red photographic plate. This is because, compared to ordinary light, the large infra red waves are much less disturbed and diverted from their path by dust particles and air molicules in the atmosphere. These researches were later followed by the discovery of the radio waves beyond the infra-red region.

Tracing Link

Based on what had been stated above, it is crystal clear that invisible infra-red has heating properties. It was been stated before that Ketu has a red and fierce look, venomous tongue, smoky colour and is a lean. The infra red rays have a heating effect and on account of the red colour as discussed in the case of Mars, these rays are more penetrating and do not bend, thus long distance photography is possible with the help of these rays. They inherit the quality of Mars and are responsible for quarrels, deception, assassinations and vicious tendencies. That is Why the term Kujavat Ketu.

Ketu is invisible with infra-red rays and it is beyond the red visible spectrum. Before coming to the world in a physical body, the astral body is invisible and physical body tries for final emancipation.

DIFFERENT CONDITIONS (AVASTHAS) OF A PLANET

1. Exalted And Debilitated Planets :

Planets	exalted	upto which degree	debilitated
Sun	Aries	10	Libra
Moon	Taurus	3	Scorpio
Mars	Capricorn	28	Cancer
Mercury	Virgo	15	Pisces
Jupiter	Cancer	5	Capricorn
Venus	Pisces	27	Virgo
Saturn	Libra	20	Aries
Rahu	Taurus	20	Scorpio
Ketu	Scorpio	20	Taurus

It is to be noted that Sun is exalted in the house where Saturn gets debilitation. Similarly Mars is exalted in the house where Jupiter gets debilitation. Venus is exalted in the house where Mercury gets debilitation. Throughout sign the planet is exalted but upto a particular degree, it is maximum exalted.

2. Mool Trikona

Mool Trikona sign of different planets is as under:

All five planets rule two signs. Sun and Moon, who own/ rule one sign each. Odd signs *i.e.* Aries, Gemini etc. are male signs and even signs like Taurus and Cancer are females signs. A planet is considered powerful in male signs except Mercury which is powerful in female sign. The Mool Trikona signs of different planets are as under :

Planet	Mool Trikona	Upto Which Degree
Mars	Aries	0-12
Mercury	Virgo	16-20
Jupiter	Saggitarious	0-18
Venus	Libra	0-15
Rahu	Gemini	–
Saturn	Aquarius	0-20
Sun	Leo	0-20
Moon	Taurus	4-20
Ketu	Saggitarious	–

3. Own House

All the planets except Sun and Moon own two signs. one male and the other female. Mars to Saturn when posited in female signs are considered as own house, except Mercury who is treated in own house in Gemini. Rahu owns Virgo and Ketu rules Pisces.

4. Combust Planets

When Mars, Mercury, Jupiter, Venus or Saturn are very close to Sun, they lose their luster (brightness) on account of nearness to the Sun. The planet is considered as deep combust, when the difference of longitude of Sun with reference to a planet is less than 3 degrees. The planets get combust when they are within the following degrees on either side of Sun.

Planet : Mars   Saturn   Mercury   Jupiter   Venus

Degree : 17   15   14   11   10

A junior officer commands the staff and he is a subordinate in front of the senior official. It is called *Vikala in* Hindi.

5. Associated

When the difference of two planets in longitude is more than 5 degrees, these planets are considered to be in associated with each other.

6. Conjunction of Planet

In a class, when there are too many students, they exert influence on each other. Similarly, there can be one or more planet(s) in a house and they influence each other. There can be conjunction of two or more planets when they are within 5 degrees from each other in a particulars house or the next house.

The degree of a planet in a particular house may be say: Libra 29, and the degree of the other planet may be 2 or 3 in Scorpio. If they are on the same longitude, it is regarded as total conjunction. The conjunction can be amongst Mars, Mercury, Jupiter, Venus and Saturn.

7. Retrograde

In Astronomical terms planets do not retrograde but the planets seem to be retrograde in relation to the earth. In fact when earth is revolving with more speed the planets seem to be going backward with relation to earth. This has been dealt with elaborately in author's book "PREDICTING EARTHQUAKE THROUGH TRASNSIT NAVAMSA". Retrograde planet is called *Shakt*.

8. Friendly Planets

The planets are considered as happy when they are in friendly houses. It works on the analogy that when we see a friend we feel happy. The Sun, the Moon and Mars are friends and Jupiter is their preceptor. Saturn, Mercury and Ketu are friends and Venus is their preceptor. It is treated as *(Mudit)* happy.

9. Inimical Planets

The first group is an enemy of the second group. When a particular planet is posited in the sign owned by the other planet, the lord of the sign may be friend or an enemy e.g. Sun in Taurus is treated as his inimical sign as Venus rules over Taurus and Sun is of the first group and Venus is of the second group. The planet when they are in the house of an enemy, they are regarded as *'Deens'* (Powerless).

10. Yogakara Planets

Yogakarka planet is that planet who owns trine and quadrant in respect of a certain Ascendant. Mars in case of Cancer Ascendant, owns the fifth house and the 10th house and in respect of Leo Ascendant, it owns quadrant and trine simultaneously and it is treated as a Yogakarka planet for Cancer and Leo Ascendants. Venus is a Yogakarka planet for the Capricorn and Aquarius Ascendant i.e. signs ruled by Saturn. Similarly Saturn become Yogkarka for Taurus and Libra Ascendants i.e. Ascendants ruled by Venus.

These planets become functional benefics and produces good results by their association or aspect with reference to the house and/or a planet. But the natural characteristics of a planet do not change, Yogakarka Saturn may take a persons to any height but he will compel him to work day and night on account of its natural characteristics.

11. Accelerated Planets

When the planets come near to the Sun, their motion increases. If the planet's motion increases than the average motion, they are treated as accelerated or *Bheet* (the state of fear). The behaviour of the accelerated planets has been discussed in detail in author's other book.

12. Stationary Planets

When the planets oppose Sun and are about 180 degrees from the Sun, their motion becomes stationary for a few days. The behaviour of stationary planets has been discussed in detail in author's other book .

CHAPTER **5**

Signs

There are 12 signs. They are ruled by different planets. Their names and lordship is indicated below. It would be noted that in the horoscope in North-India system, the number is indicated in the Horoscope. This number in fact indicates the respective sign.

	SIGNS			LORDS		
No.	English	Symbol	Hindi Equivalent	English	Symbol	Hindi Equivalent
1.	Aries	♈	Mesha	Mars	♂	Mangal
2.	Taurus	♉	Virshbha	Venus	♀	Shukra
3.	Gemini	♊	Mithuna	Mercury	☿	Budha
4.	Cancer	♋	Karaka	Moon	☽	Chandra
5.	Leo	♌	Simha	Sun	☉	Surya
6.	Virgo	♍	Kanya	Mercury	☿	Budha
7.	Libra	♎	Tula	Venus	♀	Shukra
8.	Scorpio	♏	Vrishaka	Mars	♂	Mangal
9.	Sagtitarius	♐	Dhanu	Jupiter	♃	Guru
10.	Capricorn	♑	Makra	Saturn	♄	Sani
11.	Aquarius	♒	Kumbha	Saturn	♄	Sani
12.	Pisces	♓	Meena	Jupiter	♃	Guru

The specimen of Horoscope in the North Indian style is as under :

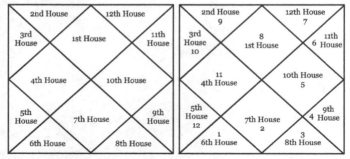

It should be noted that the house in north Indian style is immvable and the number indicated is of the sign.

Rationality

In fact, the allocation of signs is based on the motion of particular planets. Moon being the fastest planet. It takes 27 days in revolving a round the Zodiac and it is assigned the sign next to the Sun. Mercury takes 88 days and two signs. Gemini & Virgo, one from above and the other from below have been allotted to Mercury. Venus is next to Mercury and two signs Taurus and Libra, one from above and other from below are ruled by Venus. Similarly Mars, Jupiter and Saturn are assigned the signs based on their motion. Saturn is the most distant planet and is also the slowest. Two signs Capricorn and Aquarius are ruled by it.

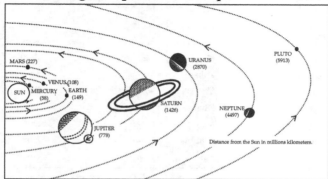

Fig. 1. *The solar systems*

PISCES	ARIES	TAURUS	GEMINI	JUPITER	MARS	VEN	MER
AQUA RIOUS			CANCER	SATURN			MOON
CAPRI CORN			LEO	SATURN			SUN
SAGTITA RIUS	SCORPIO	LIBRA	VIRGO	JUPITER	MARS	VEN	MER

Salient Features

CODE :DIRECTION :	ESWN (EAST SOUTH WEST AND NORTH)
ELEMENT :	FEAW (FIRE, EARTH, AIR & WATER)
NATURE :	MFC (MOVABLE, FIXED AND COMMON)
IN HINDI :	RISING BY HINDER PART MEANS PRISHTODAYA
	AND RISING BY HEAD IS SHIRSODAYA, PISCES IS UBHODAYA.

Fruitful/Mute Signs

Cancer, Scorpio and Pisces (all watery signs) are fruitful by nature, They are also regarded as mute signs.

Barren Sings

Aries, Gemini, Leo and Virgo are called barren or sterile signs.

Violent Signs

Signs ruled by Mars that is Aries and Scorpio are called violent signs. These signs inherit the qualities of Mars and are the best fitted to take risk.

Human signs

Gemini, Virgo Aquarius and first half of Sagtitarius are depicted by human figures and are called human signs.

Voice signs

All airy signs are also called voice signs.

Bestial Signs

Aries (ram) Taurus (bull) Leo (lion) Capricorn (goat) and 2nd half of Sagtitarius represent the figures of animals who are four legged (bestial).

Northern and Southern Signs

The first six signs of Zodiac *i.e.* Aries to Virgo are regarded as Northern signs as they are to the north of the celestial equator (Northern hemisphere). The remaining six signs of the celestial Equator (Southern hemisphere) are treated as Southern signs.

Characteristics of Different Signs

If we try to memories the characteristics of a sign, the human mind referred to as the computer will not be able to retain it and flash it back at appropriate time.

If we grasps the subject, we will not be straining ourselves and our interpretation will be accurate. Remembering too many things is a difficult process as a 'human computer' will be able to keep only the necessary data. After we grasp the system, then even without memorising, we can write the characteristics or signification of different signs based on our common knowledge. Let us take Aries. If we take the shape or symbol provide in Astrology it will be observed that the symbol of Aries is of 'ram'. Keeping the picture of ram in our mind we can easily analyse so many things about it. The ram is short statured. Its forehead is very pronounced and chin is small comparatively. It has four legs. If we see previous pages (in the tabulated form) we have indicated the directions, elements and other material studying from these, it will be observed that Aries represents east direction, is a male and fiery sign, all male signs are cruel, it too is a cruel sign. Similarly, it is a movable, odd and Prishtodaya sign.

Regarding abode or place of living if we again think about the place of living of a ram it is to be noted that rams are found in grassy lands, hilly areas, bushes, etc. Similarly, based on symbol, we can know the abode of every sign, based on this analogy we are giving a short description of each and every sign.

1. Aries

It is a male, movable, fiery, quadruped, short ascension sign and rises by hinder part. It represents East direction and rules 0 to 30 degree. It is the Mool Trikona sign of Mars. Sun is exalted and Saturn is debilitated in this sign and if the Ascendant is Aries these persons inherit natural characteristics of  Mars and are strong willed, obstinate and rash in nature.

When Aries sign rises in the Ascendant, the body description resembles Mars and the features provided to the ram that is broadheaded at temples and narrow at the chin. It should be noted that these characterstics are general in nature. They are always modified whenever there is influence of other planets either on the Ascendant. i.e. Aries sign or its lord Mars. While judging all this is to be given due weightage. A weak Mars native may suffer on account of inflammatory disease and diseases ruled by Mars. Its abode is grassy field, small hills, small bushes and small mines.

It is short statured has a broad forehead, bright eyes, stout neck and well developed body.

2. Taurus

Taurus is a female fixed, earthy, quadruped, short ascension and rises by hinder part. It represents south direction and rules 30 to 60 degree. It is ruled by Venus and inherits the natural characteristics of Venus i.e. persons will be soft spoken and well mannered. Moon and Rahu are exalted and Ketu is debilitated in this sign.

When the Taurus rises in the Ascendant the body description resembles Venus and the description indicated in respect of the symbol, short statured, broad forehead, stout neck and well built. The health of the person will depend upon influence of the malefic or benefic planet either on the Ascendant or its lord Venus. In general Taurus Ascendant born persons inherit quality of Venus. The abode of Taurus is fields, grazing, grounds, agricultural land, wet grassy land, a place where cows are kept.

3. Gemini

It is a male, airy, common, two legged, medium ascension and rises by head. It rules West

direction and rules 60 to 90 dergees. Mercury rules over this sign, who is a businessman and the persons born with the Gemini Ascendant are businessman and prove good salesman and travel agents on account of their pleasing way of talking.

The body description resembles Mercury when this sign rises in the Ascendant that is long arms, face, nose and chin. They are quick witted, but nervous and restless. Before giving any judgement the influence of malefic and benefic planets either on the Ascendant or its ord Mercury should be seen. The Gemini's abode is brothel, ball room, dancing club, cinema and gambling den.

4. Cancer

Cancer is a female, watery, rises by hinder part medium ascension sign. It represens North direction and rules 90 to 120 degree. Jupiter is exalted and Mars is debilitated in this sign.

When Cancer Ascendant rises in a native chart the body features resemble that of Moon. Round face, full cheeks. wide chest and small hands and feet. Average height and walk with a robing gait. In general the persons concerned are obsessed on account of the watery nature of this sign. A weak Moon will give disease as indicated by Moon. The abode of the Cancer is sandy place, wet fields, watery ponds, temple, a place where ladies live.

5. Leo

It is a male fiery fixed, quadruped, long ascension sign. It rises by head and rules East direction and 120 to 150 degree. It is ruled by Sun.

If the sign Leo rises in the Ascendant and Sun is strong, the person enjoys all the comforts provided to King. As the symbol of the sign is lion the person concerned will have broad shoulders large bones & muscles, thin waist statured at prominent knees. full satured and majestic appearance. Its abode is low and high lands, thick forest,

mountains, inacessible places, dangerous places, hunting grounds, lonely place and cremation grounds.

6. Virgo

It is a female, earthy common two legged and long ascension, sign. It rises by head, it rules over South direction is 150 to 180 dergee. Mercury is exalted and Venus debilitated in this sign. It is also the Mool Trikona sign of Mercury. If sign Virgo rises and Mercury is strong and well placed a person is of attractive personality and talkative, tall, dark curved hair  and eye brows, straight nose, pronounced forehead, witty and proves eleoquent speaker, salesman and travels widely for launching of the product/goods. The abode of Virgo include cinema houses, clubs, brothel houses, ship or boat.

7. Libra

It is a male, airy, movable, long ascension sign. It rises by head. It rules 180 to 210 dergee. Sun is debilitated and Saturn is exalted in this sign. It is Mool Trikina sign of Venus.

If the sign Libra rises in the ascendant it gives magnetic personality well mannered behaviour, parrot like nose, round or oval face and soft spoken. In fact it inherits the qualities of Venus. It is to be noted that the general descriptions will vary on account of influence or association of malefic or benefic planets to the ascendant or ascendant lord Venus. The abode of Libra is market place, street and racing centre etc.

8. Scorpio

Scorpio is a female, fixed watery, rising by head, long ascension sign and represents North direction. It rules 210 to 240 dergees Mars rules over this sign. Moon and Rahu are debilitated in this sign. It as an occult and mystic sign and all those who have keen interest in psychic power, this sign has such tendencies.

Scorpio limbs are well proportionate, average stature, broad face and commanding appearance. They have a flavour for jokes and enjoy the jokes in such a way that they are always serious. Like scorpio they sting and enjoy.

Its abode is at a place where insects live, holes and narrow places.

9. Sagtitarius

Sagtitarius is a male, common fiery, long ascension and rises by hinder part. It represents East direction and rules between 240 to 270 degrees.

It is Mool Trikona sign of Jupiter. When sagt itarius rises in the Ascendant, it gives well proportioned tall body and face, large forehead and long nose. It is a sign of spiritual power as the Jupiter, the planet of religion rules over this sign. The persons are blended with power of intuition and prophecy. The body structure is proportionate but theinfluence of benefic/malefic plant will modify the shape of the body. It is to be noted that influence of Saturn will keep the person thin. Similarly the influence of Mars and Sun will also keep the body thin. The influence of Jupiter as it is a planet of expansion will give obessed body.

Its abode is stable, armoury, a place where arms are manufactured or kept.

10. Capricorn

Capricorn is a female, movable, earthy, short ascension sign. It represents South direction. It rises by hinder part and rules between 270 to 300 degrees. Mars is exalted and Jupiter is debilitated in this sign. When Capricorn rises in the ascendant persons have prominent features, long nose and chin, thick neck, dark colour black hair.

Its abode is bank of river, sea, forest, lonely place, near a spider's web and cage.

11. Aquarius

Aquarius is a female fixed, short ascension sign and rising by head. It represents West direction and rules 300 to 330 degrees.

It is a Mool Trikona sign of Saturn. The symbol of this sign is one pouring out water from a round vessel or pot.

When Aquarius sign rises in the Ascendant, the appearance of the person will be strong and well formed body, oval face, handsome appearance and good looking features.

Abode of Aquarius is a place where earthern wares are kept, bushes, gambling dens, prositute houses.

12. Pisces

It is a female, common watery, short ascension rising in Ubhodaya and double legged. It represents North direction and rules between 330 to 360 degrees.

This sign is ruled by Jupiter, Venus is exalted and Mars is debilitated in this sign. The symbol is of two fishes one leading towards North and the other towards South. It is the 12th sign of Zodiac and represents mystic ideas and psychic power. It is also Moksha or Salvation sign.

Pisceans are of short stature, short limbs flashy face, soft and silky hair.

Its abode is ponds, sea, river canals, temple, ashram, places of pilgrimage.

CHAPTER 6

House

The signification of the different houses are as under :

1st House
: General nature, personality, appearance, general health etc.

  This deals with the general aspect of life.

2nd House
: Wealth, right eye, family speech.

3rd House
: Initiative, short travelling, writing, younger co-born.

4th House
: Land and property, education, mother, mind, vehicle.

5th House
: Emotions, general intelligence, children speculation, competition, love affairs.

6th House
: Debt, disease, defeat, materal uncle, sex, servant

7th House
: Partners in life, partners in business, tenant.

8th House
: Death. L.I.C. premium receivable, gratuity, pension, inheritance, mode of death, longevity.

9th House	Father, fortune, foreign travelling and deeds done in previous birth.
10th House	Profession, business service and ashram.
11th House	Gains fulfilment of the desire elder co-born.
12th House	Imprisoment, hospitalisation losses, expenditure, salvation after death.

HOUSE

Natal Horoscope

There are twelve house in a horoscope. Each house represents and influence a particular sphere of life. In this book, the signification or charateristics of a house pertatining to an individual i.e. native is being discussed. It deals with natal (or native) horoscope.

Horary Horoscope

There are many occasions when a querent has no horoscope and he visits the astrologer with a view to seek guidance. In such cases the horoscope is casted based on the time of putting the query by the querent. The significations pertaining to diffirent houses have been dealt in detail in author's other.

Political Horoscopes

These horoscopes deal with economics, social and political conditions of a country/state and are a part of Mundane Astrology. They are prepared based on the oath taking ceremony time of a political person or the time of the independence of the country. These have been further explained in author's other book.

Quadrant (Kendra) Houses

The first, fourth, seventh & tenth houses are called quadrant houses.

Trines (Trikona) Houses

The fifth and ninth houses are called trines or trikona.

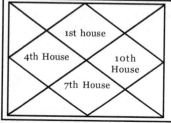
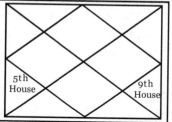

Succeedent (Panapras) Houses

The second, eight and eleventh houses are treated as succeedent.

Candent (Apoklims) House

The third, the sixth and the twelveth houses are regarded as cadent houses.

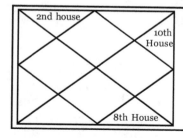
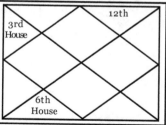

Trik (Dusthtan) Houses

The sixth, eight and twelfth house are called trik houses.

Upchaya

The third, sixth, tenth and eleventh houses are called upchaya.

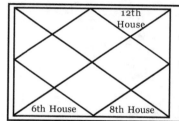
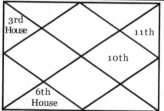

Nature of House

The house have been divided as auspicious, inauspicious and neutral. Trik houses are inauspicious while all other houses are auspicious except the third house which is neutral. The auspicious houses have been shown as Melon and inauspicious as knife/dagger. These will be discussed in subsequent pages.

CHAPTER 7

Aspect

Planets influence the house or the other planets either through aspect or through association/position. In layman's language aspect means to see and the word 'posited' means position of a planets in a particular house. The particular house is influenced either by aspect in a particular house. The particular house is influenced either by aspect of a planet or the position of a planet. We see in our daily life that the child comes to our lap if through eyes (aspect) he feels that he will be welcomed. The child may come and may immediately go back if he observes through the eyes that his visit is not welcome. On this analogy, the planets(s) influence(s) the house/planets through aspect.

The aspect is of two types, full or partial. All the planets aspect the 7th house from their position. It is called full aspect. Similarly Jupiter, Rahu and Ketu have special aspect of the 5th and the 9th from its position. Saturn aspects 3rd and 10th from its position. Mars special aspect is 4th and the 8th.

The difference between the aspect of different planets shall be such that the planet will pass on its natural characteristics as indicated in chapter-4, to the house either through aspect or through position. The difference of aspect between the Mars and Saturn will be that the position or the association or the aspect of Saturn will inculcate a habit of delay and it will try to delay all types of events. In case of Mars, it will pass on its basic natural characteristics of bruteness, aggression, rashness etc. Mars will believe that work should be done within a short span. The basic characteristics of Rahu is that it is a planet of deception. either it exposes any secret action or hides an events. The association or the aspect of Rahu shall inculcate and mould the event in such a way that person concerned may become instrumental in a fraud. The basic characteristics of Jupiter is to provide blessings and through such blessings there is expansion because the aspect of Jupiter shall create an atmosphere of expansion. The aspect of benefic planet shall be beneficial for the particular house.

Though the aspect of Mars and Saturn is considered bad on account of their natural characteristics but in case of Cancer and Leo Ascendant, Mars owns quadrant and trine. Similarly in respect of Taurus and Libra Ascendants Saturn rules qudrant and trine. Then the aspect of Mars and Saturn becomes beneficial on account of the functional nature of Mars and Saturn which they acquire on account of the reason that they become Yogakarka. Yoga means addition and Karka (significator) means one who helps in fulfillment of desire.

CHAPTER **8**

Rationality in Sequence of Days

H ora originally formed part to the terms AHORATRA which stands for day and night. It is a measure of time and by dropping initial 'A' and terminal 'TRA' we derive the word Hora.

There are 24 Horas in a day and so are 24 hours. The English word hour seems to be product of our word Hora. On each day (Sunday etc.) the first Hora is for that planet followed by other Horas. The first Hora is calculated after sunrise.

The sequence of Sunday to Saturday has been arrived as under:

The speed of different planets to go around the Zodiac which consist of 360° is as below:

S.No.	Planets	Time
1	Saturn	29.46 yr
2	Jupiter	11.86 yr
3	Mars	688 days
4	Sun (Earth)	365 days
5	Venus	225 days
6	Mercury	88 days
7	Moon	27 days

Based on speed a chart is drawn, 1st hora of the day starts with the day itself for example - Saturday–1st hora is ruled by Saturn followed by Jupiter, Mars, Sun, Venus, Mercury and Moon. The days have a very scientific origin based on planetary influence. The chart illustrates this clearly.

Chart is based on Motion of planets commencing from slowest to fastest. It indicates the sequence of days from Sunday to Saturday.

Saturn	Jupiter	Mars	Sun	Venus	Mercury	Moon
1	2	3	4	5	6	7
8	9	10	11	12	13	14
15	16	17	18	19	20	21
22	23	24	1 Sunday	2	3	4
5	6	7	8	9	10	11
12	13	14	15	16	17	18
19	20	21	22	23	24	1 Monday
2	3	4	5	6	7	8
9	10	11	12	13	14	15
16	17	18	19	20	21	22
23	24	1 Tuesday	2	3	4	5
6	7	8	9	10	11	12
13	14	15	16	17	18	19
20	21	22	23	24	1 Wednesday	2
3	4	5	6	7	8	9
10	11	12	13	14	15	16
17	18	19	20	21	22	23
24	1 Thursday	2	3	4	5	6
7	8	9	10	11	12	13
14	15	16	17	18	19	20
21	22	23	24	1 Friday	2	3
4	5	6	7	8	9	10
11	12	13	14	15	16	17
18	19	20	21	22	23	24
1 Saturday	2	3	4	5	6	7
8	9	10	11	12	13	14
15	16	17	18	19	20	21
22	23	24	1 Sunday			

* Sun Represents Earth.

CHAPTER 9

Significator

In judgement of a horoscope, what we require is the strength of a planet, the house and the significator for the house that is HKL. where H stands for house K for Karak or significator and L for Lord of the house If we want to judge the possibility of a marriage we have to weigh the strength of the 7th house, its lord and the significator for the 7th house.

In fact, if the house is weak say if the 4th house is weak it does not mean that all affairs connected with the 4th house will become weak. To avoid such a situation our sages coined different significators for different houses. In respect of the 4th house, Moon is a significator for mother and mental peace, Mars is a significator for property, Venus is a significator for vehicle, Jupiter is significator for education. In other words on account of the weak 4th house and weak lord of the 4th house together with weak Moon which is a significator for mother, the child may lose the mother but he may enjoy the benefits if Venus is strong, may be well educated if Jupiter is strong etc.

The role of a significator in astrology is very vital. The significator (Karak) for different houses are as under :

Ascendant	Sun
2nd House	Jupiter for wealth, Mercury for speech, Sun for right eye.
3rd House	Mars for younger coborn, Mercury for writing and travelling, Moon for frequent travelling.
4th House	Moon for mother and mental peace, Mars for landed property, Jupiter for education, Venus for vehicles, Sun for fame.
5th House	Jupiter for children, Mercury for speculation or shares. It is a house of devotion also, Mars will take the person towards the worship of Lord Hanuman. Female planets indicate worship of female deity and male for male deity.
6th House	Mars.
7th House	Venus for sex, Jupiter for spouse.
8th House	Saturn
9th House	Jupiter for worship and travelling to religious places, Venus for foreign travelling, Sun for father.
10th House	Sun for politics fame and Govt. favour, Mercury for trading, Saturn for Industry, Different planets will try to take to the business/profession according to their natural properties.
11th House	Jupiter for finance, Mercury for shares.
12th House	Saturn for hospitalisation, Mars for injury, Moon for left eye.

CHAPTER **10**

A Brief Description of Astronomical Terms

1. Aphelion - The point on a planetary orbit at which a body is farther from the Sun. The Sun's radius vector is the longest at this point. Helion means Sun.

2. Apogee - The point in its orbit around the earth when a body is at the greatest distance from the Earth.

3. Conjunction - The position whereby who celestial objects are lined up with each other as seen from Earth. A planet is at a superior conjunction when situated at the other side of the Sun as seen from Earth and at inferior conjunction when located directly between the Sun and Earth.

4. Declination - The angular distance between a celestial object and the celestial Equator. It is measured along the hour circle passing through the celestial body.

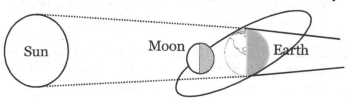

Fig. 1

5. Eclipse - The total obscuration of one celestial body by another. An eclipse of the Sun occurs when the moon passes directly between it and the Earth. An eclipse of the Moon takes place when the Earth passes between the Sun and Moon, and the Earth's shadow is thrown on to the lunar surface.

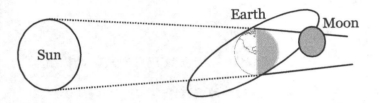

Fig. 2

6. Ecliptic–The apparent path of the Sun through the Sky during the course of a year. It is a great circle cutting the celestial equator at an angle of about 23½°. The angle varies between 21.50' to 24-36'. It is regarded as obliquity of the eclipse.

Equinoctical Points

The points at which the ecliptic and the celestial equator intersect each other at two points. This happens twice a years as the Sun crosses the equator. These are known as Vernal Equinox (March) and Autumnal Equinox (September). Vernal equinox is the point at which the ecliptic crosses the celestial as the Sun passes from South to North. At this time, the apparent longitude of the Sun is 0°. Autumnal equinox. is the point at which the ecliptic crosses he celestial equator as the Sun passes from North to South, the apparent longitude of the sun is 180°. At these times day and night are equal.

7. Equator–It is an imaginary line running round the Earth which divides the Earth into Northern hemisphere and Southern hemisphere.

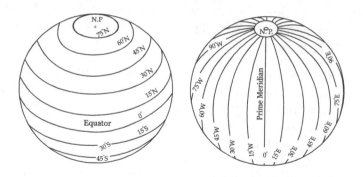

Fig. 3. *Latitudes and longitudes*

8. Inferior planet–A planet which travels around the Sun
    in an orbit inside that of the Earth. The planets
    Mercury and Venus are treated as Inferior planets.

9. Mean Solar – Mean Solar time is a measuring time
    based on the diurnal motion of the fictitious mean
    Sun, assuming that the rate of rotation of earth is
    constant.

10. Occultation–The passage of the one celestial body in
    front of another as seen from Earth occurs when
    Moon passes in front of a star or a planet. An eclipse
    is a type of occultation.

11. Opposition - The point at which a superior planet is
    directly opposite to the Sun in the sky and which is
    therefore due South at midnight. At the time of such
    a phenomena the apparent celestial longitude of two
    bodies differs by 180°.

12. Orbit–The path of one object around another.

13. Penumbra-The area of partial shadow which appears
    during a solar eclipse and which is seen to surround
    the umbra or darker central region of shadow.

14. Perigee–The point in its orbit around the Earth that a
    body is at its least distance to the Earth.

15. Perihelion–The point at its orbit at which a body is nearest to the Sun. The Sun's radius vector is shortest at this point.

16. Precession-At the time of Vernal equinox when the Sun is 0 degree Aries, the day and night are equal. At that time, the position of the Earth in reference to the fixed star is nearly 50" of space farther west then the earth was at the same equinoctial movement of the previous years. It happens on account of the gravitational pull of the Sun, Moon and Earth. But in addition to this, the entire solar system is subject to this westward motion. This equatorial bulge produces a wobble in the Earth axis similar to that of a spinning top which is slowing down and is regarded as the precession of the Equinoxes.

17. Superior planet–A planet that travels around the Sun in an orbit outside that of the Earth. Mars, Jupiter, Saturn Pluto etc. are treated as superior planet.

18. Solstice–The time of solstices are those at which the Sun's apparent longitude is 90° (Summer solstice) and 270° (Winter solstice). At summer solstice, the day is longest and at winter solstice, the day is shortest for observers in the northern hemisphere.

CHAPTER 11

Rahu and Undiagnosed Disease

It has amply been made clear that the rays of Rahu are invisible. They affect the mankind secretly. As such when the person's concerned Rahu sub period or sub period is in operation, on account of presence of these rays in the body, if the person suffers on account of some disease, during this period, the rays of Rahu (Ultra Violet) do not allow the medicine its full effect as they act as an obstructing agent (Sanivat Rahu) and there is too much delay in curing the person as had already been explained that Saturn is a planet of delay or obstruction and the ultra violet rays are more penetrating. These ultra violet rays are present in the person's body if Rahu's sub period or sub sub-period is in operation. According to the law of nature, the red rose looks red as it absorbs all the colours and repels only red colour. It is based on Newton's law of '*Similar poles repel each other*'. Based on this principle, the ultra violet rays present in the body repel the X-rays at the time of x-ray and the x-ray report is negative, though the person has been suffering all along. These ultra violet rays present in the body do not allow the pathological test to show the correct picture and the pathological reports are always negative. The person goes from one doctor to another doctor but the disease is not cured.

The person after trying medical science takes the helps of the other sciences like spiritual healing or consulting an astrologer. The Mantra rays generated by a spiritualist on account of continuous recitation of the Mantra and the ultra violet rays available from the universe work on the same wave length and the spiritual healing had no effect as the ultra violet rays hinders the Mantra rays also. They strike and finish. At this time, the sufferer goes to an astrologer. Rahu sub period commences first in the life of a person thereafter followed by the Jupiter period. During Rahu period he contacts cheats, whether spiritual, medical or astrologer and thereby he loses his money.

Though he is frustrated but this necessity compels him to one door after the other. He continues to knock the doors till such time the Rahu period is in operation. During this periods, if a person consults a genuine astrologer also, the obstructing ultra violet rays do not allow the astrologer to assess the horoscope correctly and he misjudges it.

Thereafter Jupiter period commences. Jupiter is planet of divine grace and he contacts a genuine person, but by this time he has lost all the hopes but forced by circumstances he consults him.

Controlling Ultra Violet Rays

Astrology without astral remedies is like a body without a soul. Sage Parasar had laid much stress on astral remedies. He had prescribed remedies such as feeding the needy persons, wearing of Gems, Yantra recitation of the tantric mantra of a particular planet and taking bath with the medicinal herbs. All these have been dealt in the author's book "Experiments in Remedial Measures". The logic behind charity is that the particular rays are repelled and the sufferers get relief. Our sages who were peerless scientists observed the effects of different wavelength and based on that were able to decide the wavelength of different products and they prescribed the donation of these products to the needy persons. It had a dual effect. The miseries of the persons are reduced as the sub conscious part of the soul definitely blesses the donor and he is relieved of his problems. It is very difficult to part off one's wealth but once, one who takes interest in feeding the poor, he never look back as he gets much more benefits than the amount spent. In Moon's chapter it has been indicated, with the supports of modern science, as to how we have arrived at the conclusion that water, milk, curd, cream, butter and ghee ruled by Moon and they repel the Moon's rays.

It is advised that if a disease remains undiagnosed for a considerable period, the sufferer should first perform the remedies of Rahu and after that he should go for different test. As a charity, coconut is offered in Shri Ganesh temple in Bombay and other temples. Radish which represent Rahu is offered in temple in Belur Math in Calcutta, Halwa and the Prasad offered in many South Indian temples is also of the products ruled by Rahu, After distributing Halwa to the needy persons, if an x-ray is taken, it will show the correct disease and thereby the correct treatment.

CHAPTER 12

Functional Benefics
and Malefics

Saturn, Mars, Sun, Rahu & Ketu are considered natural malefics. Moon, Jupiter, Venus and Mercury are natural benefics. But in certain cases Saturn, Mars and Sun become functional benefics. This can be explained with the help of an example. Poison kills a person. But in case of a person bitten by a snake, poison in injected to him. This poison now saves the person. The natural characteristic of poison is to harm a person but the functional characteristic is that it saves the person. So in certain circumstances natural malefics may act like functional benefics. Similarly natural benefics when they are lords of the 6th, 8th or 12th house becoomes functional malefics . Sage Parasar had said.

(i)   The lords of the 9th and the 5th houses are auspicious.

(ii) The Lords of the 6th, the 8th or the 12th are inauspicious.

(iii) The lords of quandrant, if natural benefics, do not give benefic reults,

(iv) The lords of quadrant, if malefics, do not give malefic results.

(v) The lords of the 11th is most malefic.

According to the author's experience, the lords of the quadrant, if they are natural benefic, give benefic results. It may be on account of some other reason that the person may have suffered. The Panch Maha Purush Yoga arises when Jupiter or Mercury is posited in its own house in a quadrant. These are called Hans and Bhandra Yoga respectively Sage Parasar had considered lord of the 11th house as most malefic on account of the reason that the 11th house is the house of income and a rich person does not understand the difficulties faced by the poor. There is a saying "Kanak Kanak se soo guni madakata adhikay" Kanak means belladona which gives intoxication and Kanak also means gold. That is gold is more intoxicating than the natural intoxicating Kanak (Belladona). On account of this Sage Parasar had considered it as malefic. But money is the source of all comfort and no one can afford to do anything without it. The 11th lord is not malefic but the quality of wealth is that the holder does not give attention to other persons. There are two signs owned by each planet except Sun and Moon who own one sign each. One of the signs ruled by Mars, Mercury, Jupiter Venus and Saturn is more powerful than the other. This powerful sign is the mool trikona sign of the planet. The mool trikona signs of Mars, Mercury, Jupiter, Venus and Saturn are Aries, Virgo, Sagt itarius Libra and Aquarius. These signs are more powerful than their other signs. Due weightage has to be given when Saturn rules over the 6th & 7th house in case of Leo Ascendant or the 7th or the 8th in case of Cancer Ascendant or the 8th and the 9th house in case of Gemini Ascendant. Similarly Jupiter can also be lord of the 6th and the 9th house, in case of Cancer Ascendant. In such a condition, it is to be treated as functional malefic though Jupiter is a natural benefic.

Ascendantwise benefics and malefics.

Aries–Jupiter and Sun are benefics on account of the lord of the 9th and the 5th house respectively. Mars is benefic being lord of the Ascendant. There are two signs of a planet. A planet is more powerful in its mool trikona sign. Mars is 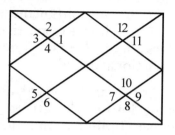 benefics as its more powerful signs falls in the Ascendant, Mercury, though natural benefics, is functional malefics being lord of the 6th house.

Taurus–Jupiter and Mars are functional malefics being lords of the 8th and the 12th house respectively lords of the 8th and the 12th house respectively. Venus owns the 6th house and treated as neutral being lord of the Ascendant also. Saturn will be 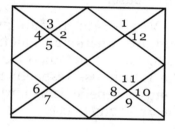 most benefic as it is Yogakaraka on account of the reason it is lord of 9th house and 10th house being trine and quadrant.

Gemini–Venus and Saturn are benefics. No functional malefic for this Ascendant.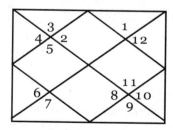

Cancer–Jupiter, Saturn and Mercury are functional malefics being lords of the 6th, 8th & 12th house respectively. Mars is a yogakaraka. Venus is a functional benefic.

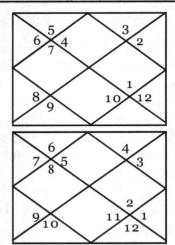

Leo–Mars is a yogakaraka being lord of the 4th & 9th house, Jupiter is functional benefic being lord of the 5th house, Sagtitarius is powerful than Pisces, Moon is functional malefic being the lord of the 12th house.

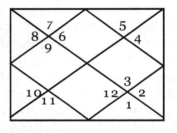

Virgo–Saturn, Mars and Sun are functional malefics being lord of the 6th, 8th and the 12th house respectively. Venus is benefic being lord of the 9 and 2nd house.

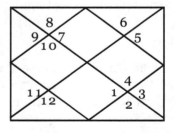

Libra–Saturn   is   a yogakaraka and Mercury is malefic being lord of the 12th house which is its powerful sign.

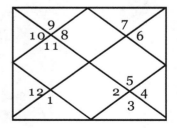

Scorpio–Jupiter, Sun and Moon are functional benefics. Venus is a functional malefic. Mars is treated as neutral as it is lord of the Ascendant.

Saggitarius–Sun and Mars are benefics, Moon is malefic being lord of the 8th house.

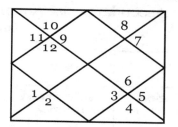

Capricorn–Jupiter and Sun are functional malefics being lord of 8th house and 12th house. Venus is a yogakarka being lord of 5th house and 10th house Mercury is a functional benefic being lord of 9th house.

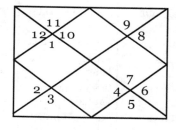

Aquarius–Moon and Mercury are malefics being the lord of the 6th and the 8th house respectively Venus is a yogakaraka being lord of 4th and 9th house. Jupiter is a benefic.

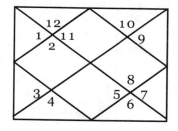

Pisces–Sun, Venus and Saturn are functional malefics being lord of 6th, 8th and 12th house respectively. Moon and Mars are respectively lords of 5th house and 9th house and are functional benefic.

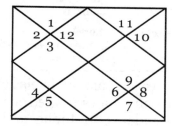

Ascendant-wise Auspicious Days, Colours And Stones

	Days	Colours	Stones
Aries	Tuesday, Sunday and Thursday	Red, purple yellow	Red coral, ruby and Yellow sapphire.
Taurus	Saturday Wednesday	Black & green	blue Sapphire, Emerald
Gemini	Saturday, Friday Wednesday	Black, steel grey, green	Blue sapphire, diamond, emerald
Cancer	Tuesday, Monday	Red, white	Red, coral, pearl
Leo	Sunday, Tuesday Thursday	Purple, red Yellow	Ruby, red, coral sapphire sapphire
Virgo	Wednesday Thursday	Green, yellow	Emerald, yellow sapphire
Libra	Friday, Monday Saturday	Cream, black White	Diamond, blue Sapphire, pearl
Scorpio	Monday, Sunday Thursday & Tuesday	White, yellow, purple, red	Pearl yellow sapphire, ruby, red coral
Sagtitarius	Thursday, Wednesday, Tuesday, Sunday	Yellow green purple, red	Yellow sapphire emerald, ruby, red coral
Capricorn	Saturday, Friday Wednesday	Black, Cream green	Blue sapphire diamond, emerald
Aquarius	Friday, Saturday Tuesday & Thursday	Cream Black Red yellow	Diamond, blue sapphire, red coral yellow sapphire
Pisces	Thursday, Monday, Tuesday Wednesday	Yellow green White, red	Yellow sapphire emeald pearl red coral

The rationality in classification of auspicious colours, days and stones is based on the auspicious planets. For Aries Ascendant Sun, Jupiter and Mars rule over the 5th, 9th and the Ascendant. Sunday, Thursday and Tuesday have been treated as auspicious. Sun rules over ruby, Jupiter rules over yellow sapphire and Mars over red coral.

The day, colour and stone for each planet is as under :

Sun	Sunday	Purple	Ruby
Moon	Monday	White	Pearl
Mars	Tuesday	Red	Red coral
Mercury	Wednesday	Green	Emerald
Jupiter	Thursday	Yellow	Yellow sapphire
Venus	Friday	Cream	Diamond
Saturn	Saturday	Blue	Blue sapphire
Rahu	Saturday	Smoky grey	Gomedh
Ketu	Tuesday	Deep red	Turquoise

Ascendantwise inauspicious days, colours and stones are as under. The rationality in choosing the colour is based on the functional malefics for each ascendant.

Ascendant	Days	Colours	Stones
1. Aries	Wednesday	Green	Emerald
2. Taurus	Tuesday, Thursday	Yellow, red	Yellow sapphire red coral
3. Gemini	—	—	—
4. Cancer	Thursday Saturday	Yellow, black	Blue and yellow sapphire
5. Leo	Monday	White	Pearl
6. Virgo	Saturday, Tuesday, Sunday	Black, red purple	Blue sapphire red coral, ruby
7. Libra	Thursday Wednesday	Yellow Green	Emerald, yellow sapphire
8. Scorpio	Friday	Cream	Diamond
9. Sagtittarius	Monday	White	Pearl
10. Capricorn	Monday Sunday Thursdays	Yellow Purple	Ruby, yellow sapphire
11. Aquarius	Monday Wednesday	White, green	Pearl emerald
12. Pisces	Sunday, Friday, Saturday	Purple, cream black	Ruby, blue sapphire diamond

CHAPTER 13

Strength of Planet

Varahmihir and other writers had paid much attention on the strength of the planets. The following are ten conditions of planetary strengths.

1. Exalted (*Deeptha*)–When a planet is exalted it is regarded as Deeptha. It provides gains of conveyance, fame respect from elders etc.

2. Health (*Swastha*)–When a planet is in its own sign, it is to be treated as Swastha or in a healthy condition. Its results are fame, wealth, position and good progeny.

3. Happy (*Mudit*)–A planet which is in the house of its friend is happy *(Mundit).* It provides happiness.

4. Tranquil *(Shanta)*–Is the condition of a planet when it is auspicious vargas. It provides strength, courage, conforts and happiness.

5. Retrogression *(Shakta)*–When a planet is in retrogression, it is treated as Shakta. It showers reputation, wealth and good progeny according to classics. But according to the author's

experience, it becomes detrimental even if it is posited in its own house.

6.   Inimical *(Deena)*–A planet posited in inimical house is treated as deen and is responsible for mental worry, brain trouble and degradation.

7.   Combustion *(Vikala)*–When a planet is very near to the Sun, it gets combust *i.e.* loses its own luster. A combust planet brings disease, loss of wife and children and disgrace.

8.   Residence in the last quarter of a sign *(Peedya)*–A planet in the last quarter of a sign is regarded as peedya and has a tendency for criminal prosecution, pilfering habits and expulsion from the country.

9.   Debilitated *(Khala)*–A debilitated planet is responsible for losses, quarrel with presents and relations, imprisonment and trouble from various sources.

10. Acceleration *(Bheeta)*–It is a very rare phenomena when planets acquire more than their usual speed. It signifies losses, misfortune, and foes.

The planets have also been allotted five stages of life. In the odd sign they are:

1.   Childhood–When a planet is upto 5 degree, it is treated as a child.

2.   Boyhood–A planet upto 10 degree is treated as boy

3.   Young–A planet between 10 to 20 degree is regarded as young.

4.   Old–A planet above 20 degree upto 25 degree is regarded as old.

5.   Very Old–A planet more than 25 degree is considered very old.

The result accrues according to age. In even signs, the system is reversed *i.e.* first 5 signifies very old and so on.

Shadbala or Six Sources of Strength

1. Positional strength–A planet gets the position strength as a result of occupying a house of exhalation, mooltrikona, its own house or when in a friend's house.

2. Directional strength–It is the strength which a planet acquires when it is in a particular direction. Jupiter and Mercury are powerful in the Ascendant (East) Sun and Mars in 10th house (south) Saturn in 7th house (West) and Venus and Moon get their directional strength in 4th house (North)

3. Time strength–This refers to strength acquired by a planet according to time Kala (a) Moon, Mars and Saturn are powerful during night. Sun, Jupiter and Venus are powerful during day. Mercury is always powerful. (b) Malefics are powerful during the dark half and benefics during bright half of the lunar month (c) Mercury is powerful at sunrise. Sun in the noon. Jupiter at mid-day. Saturn in the evening, Moon in the first part of the night, Venus at mid night and Mars in the last part of night. (d) Planets are powerful during their week days, that is Sun is powerful on Sunday Moon on Monday and so on. (e) Similarly planets are powerful in their Hora. The first Hora at the time of sunrise is of the planet ruling the day i.e. on Sunday the first Hora is of Sun followed by the Hora of the planet as mentioned in another chapter. (f) Planets are powerful in a particular season. Sun is powerful during summer and so is Mars. Moons is powerful in rainy season, Mercury in Sarat season, Jupiter in Hemant season, Venus in Spiring season and Saturn in Winter season.

4. Aspectional strength–Aspect of a natural benefic planet will boost up the affairs of that house and aspect of a natural malefic planet destroys the indications of that house. The aspect of Yogakaraka Saturn and Mars will be beneficial. A planet is a Yogakaraka when it is the lord of a quadrant and a trine. Saturn in case of Taurus Ascendant is the lord of 9th and 10th house and in case of Libra Ascendant is the lord of 4th and 5th house and as such its aspect will be beneficial. Similarly in Cancer and Leo Ascendant, Mars is a Yogakaraka planet and its aspect is benefic.

5. Natural strength–It is the natural strength of a planet. Sun is most powerful followed by Moon, Venus, Jupiter, Mercury, Mars and Saturn which is the least powerful. The strength of Mars is double than that of Saturn's Mercury is four times stronger than Mars. Jupiter is eight times stronger than that of Mercury. Venus has eight times more strength than that of Jupiter. Moon is sixteen times stronger than Venus, the Sun twice of the Moon and Rahu's strength is twice that of the Sun's and hence Rahu is the strongest of all planets.

6. Motional strength–Sun and Moon are powerful in Sun's northerly course. The signs Capricorn to Gemini constitute Sun's northerly course. Mars, Mercury, Jupiter, Venus and Saturn are powerful in retrogression or in conjunction with full Moon when they acquire motional strength. If Jupiter, Mercury, Venus and Saturn are with Mars they are said to be defeated in planetary fight and get motional strength. According to author's experience a retrograde planet acts like the reverse gear of the vehicle. A retrograde planet in it own house becomes detrimental to the house. A retrograde planet is like a person going out of his house.

An external planet when in opposition to the Sun is nearest to the earth and at the same time retrograde too. The planet on account of its nearness to the earth and has a strongest magnetic and gravitational pull on the earth. The inferior planet *viz*. Mercury and Venus, when they are nearest to the earth, exert strongest influence on earth. At such a time they are retrograde also. As such these planets have strongest gravitational pull on the earth. That is how retrograde planets are considered strong. The Sun has the biggest mass in our solar system.

As per the law of gravity, the gravitational pull of the Sun will be more on the earth and it will affect the earth maximum. The gravitational force between the two bodies is directly proportional to the square of the distance between the two. This can be worked out as under :

$$F = \frac{M_1 \times M_2}{d_2}$$

Where F is the force of attraction between two masses. M_1 and M_2 and d is the distances between the two (from centre to centre). The gravitational force between a planet and the earth shall be :

$$\frac{M\,P \times M\,E}{d\,2}$$

Where MP is the mass of the planet and ME is the mass of the earth and d is the distance between the two.

As such the maximum effect of a planet on the earth will be when it is nearest to the earth. This happens on account of the reason that the distance between the earth and the planet shall be minimum. The minimum the distance of the planet from the earth, the maximum will be pull of the planet on the earth. Rationality, *that is why retrograde planets are considered strong.*

CHAPTER 14

Principle for Interpretation

A t the time of the examination of an horoscope due attention has to been given to the strength/weakness of the house, its lord and the significator of the house. Navamsa and other charts are to be given due weightage. The basic principles based on astrological cannons are :

(a)   'NANAK DUKHIYA SAB SANSARA' Guru Nanak says all the people are suffering. There are five malefic planets Rahu, Ketu, Saturn, Mars and Sun. There are twelve houses. These planets will occupy one or the other house and will spoil the houses where they have a influence by way of aspect/ position.

(b)   'APNI GALI MAY KUTTA BHE SHER HOTA HAI' Even the dog enjoys the power of a lion in his two house. That house is strong which is aspected/posited by its own lord and such a planet will promote the affairs ruled by that house. In case of a retrograde planet, the retrograde planet becomes detrimental to the house and does not support it.

(c) 'KHARBOOJA CHAKU PAR GIRE YA CHAKU
     KHARBOJJE PAR GIRE. KATATA KHARBOOJA
     HE HAY' Whether the melon (Kharbooja) fall on
     a knife (chaku) or knife falls on the melon, the
     harm is only to the melon. Houses 6th, 8th and
     12th are inauspicious (Knife) and the remaining
     houses are auspicious. Lords of the 6th, the 8th
     and the 12th spoil the indication of the house where
     they are posited and any planet which joins these
     house also loses its vitality.

(d) 'WHEN TWO BULLS FIGHT THEY SPOIL THE
     CROP' Two or more than two malefic planets
     associated with a house weaken the signification
     of that house.

(e) 'CHALTI CHAKKI DEKH KAR DIYA KABIRA
     ROI, DO PATAN KE BICH MAY SABUT BACHA
     NE KOY' If the house is hemmed in between two
     malefics, it loses is vitality, like the two wheels of
     the grinding machine which grinds grain. Such a
     weak house promotes the affairs of that house to
     a very limited extent. Suppose the 5th house is
     hemmed in between malefics there may be delay
     in getting progeny and if the progeny is granted
     the person may not enjoy satisfaction though
     them.

(f) The house will prosper if it is aspected by the benefic
     planet(s).

(g) The house aspected or associated with malefic
     planet(s) will lose vitality, Malefic planets are weak
     Moon, Sun, Mars, Rahu, Saturn and Ketu.
     Mercury in conjunction with a malefic will give
     the result of a malefic.

(h) Close association of planets. In the chapter
     "Strength of a planet" Rahu and Ketu have been
     shown as the most powerful. Any planet which is

very close to them loses its vitality, the more the closeness the more the miseries. Total conjunction is very harmful. The total conjunction is when the degree of two planets are equal and they are posited in a house or the malefic aspects from some other house. A closeness of Saturn with any planet will delay/deprive the event(s) connected with that house or the properties of that planet. Saturn closely associated with Moon will bring too much depression to a person. In case of a lady there will be irregularity in the periods too. Any planet which is very close to Sun loses its vitality. Combust planets are like the burnt roti/bread. The more the bread is burnt, the little salvage value it has. The more the closeness of Sun to Moon, Mars, Mercury, Jupiter, Venus and Saturn, the more is the damage concerning the significations ruled by that planet.

The planets give maximum result, positive or negative in their main periods, and sub periods. In their sub sub periods, together with the help of 'Transits' the actual date of the happening can be worked out. The lords of the 9th and the 5th house promote the affairs connected with the house provided they are not rendered weak on account of one of the above reasons. The Lord of the 6th, the 8th or the 12th house do not give good results in their sub periods, and sub sub periods, planets which are 6/8 to each other or 2/12 to each other try to create problems connected with those houses.

Let us apply these rules to Sh. Ram's horoscope. The Ascendant is Cancer. Its lord Moon is posited in the Ascendant and is associated with the Jupiter who is the lord of the 6th house. It is aspected by exalted Saturn, Mars and Ketu. Exalted Jupiter associated with ascendant lord Moon is responsible for Gaj Kesari Yoga, a yoga which provides general prosperity. It indicates that the person should have faith in religion should be pious and man of principle. Exalted Jupiter in the Ascendant causes 'Hams Yoga'

Jupiter is also a functional malefic on account of its ownership of the 6th house and is aspecting Scorpio, the 5th house, Capricorn the 7th house and the Pisces the 9th house. According to natural characteristics of Jupiter the children, the wife, the father and the precepter all should be devoted to God. But Jupiter does not spare them on account of the reason that it becomes a functional malefic on account of its ownership of the 6th house. The 6th house represents hidden enemy. In the initial stage Ravana was a hidden enemy. Being lord of the 6th house (enemy) (Sh. Ram's enemy was not only pious but very powerful also) (Jupiter exalted) the 6th lord in the Ascendant, (See Chaku Kharbooja per gira).

Mars is aspecting the Ascendant, this makes the native a very powerful person. Exalted Mars in the 7th house is responsible for Ruchaka Yoga. Mars is also aspecting where powerful exalted Sun is posited. This gave Shri Ram all the powers, But exalted Saturn, which is a planet of delay and frustration, is aspecting the 10th house (Aries) the 6th house and the Ascendant. Exalted Saturn in the quadrant causes Sasa yoga. Saturn by nature is a planet of delay, its intensity increases on account of its, *exaltness*. Saturn is *retrograde. It shows exit.* Sh. Ram had go to the forest, the day he was to be crowned as a king. Saturn did not allow him the crown for fourteen years (a planet of delay). Saturn withdrew all the facilities which are afforded to a king. Exalted Saturn in the house of property indicates that he had vast property but retrograde planet who is also lord of the 8th house (knife) withdrew the benefits accruing to him with this property. Retrograde Saturn did not allow the crown on account of its aspect on the 10th house and the significator for the 10th house Sun. The aspect of retrograde Saturn on the 6th house did not spare Ravana also and he was deprived of all the property. Saturn is aspecting the 6th house and its lord Jupiter.

Saturn is also the lord of the 7th house. Jupiter and Moon, two natural benefics are aspecting the house of marriage.

Exalted Mars is posited in the house of marriage. Sita had the qualities of Jupiter and Mars. Retrograde Saturn in the first instance took her to the forest, secondly she was separated from Ram and tortured by Ravana. When she came back she was again sent to the forest on account of the criticism by the royal washerman. Saturn is slow poisonous planet. Manthra slowly poisoned Kaikae. Exalted Saturn indicates royal servant. Manthra and the washerman were the royal servants. Saturn represents servant. Exalted Saturn meand servant to a royal family. So, Manthra was responsible for the exile of Shri Ram. Mars is aspecting the Ascendant. He inherited the qualities of Mars and he was courageous, powerful and a strong warrior.

The 3rd house (Virgo) represents co-born. Its lord Mercury is posited in the house of gains. Sh. Ram's all younger brothers helped him a lot. Exalted Venus with Ketu is posited in the house of fortune, foreign and father. His father was a great king on account of the presence of exalted Venus. The lord of the 9th house jupiter is also exalted. This shows the strength of the father.

A special chapter has been given in one of author's book which indicates the results of the mutual aspect of Ketu and Jupiter. Mutual aspect of Jupiter and Ketu is responsible for using the Mantra Shakti against the person. Ravana and his son had to make use of the Mantra Shakti to give harm to Shri Ram. He was successful on many occassions when his son Meghnad used a mantra arrow against lord Hanuman and the snake shakti against Shri Ram and Laxman. Thereafter he was not allowed to regenerate that Mantra shakti, Rahu and Ketu are invisible. Ketu represents a secret plot and Venus is the significator for the wife. Ravana kidnapped Sitaji. In the 9th house Venus is posited. Venus represents South East direction and Shri Ram had to go towards the south direction in search of his wife.

Ravana was a secret enemy till he was not traced. He became an open enemy thereafter. The 7th house represents the known enemy. Retrograde Saturn representing the 7th house, the house of open enemy, did not spare Ravana and he had to lose everything including his life. Exalted Sun in the house of profession indicates a man of fame and power. Aspect of Saturn on Sun (significator for father) also frustrated the father.

Dasarath got sons at the fag end of his life, that too after performing a yagna (ritual). The 9th house represents father. In Sh. Ram horoscope Pisces Sign is in the 9th house. Treating it as Ascendant, let us recast this chart.

Let us analyse the 5th house. The 5th house is Cancer and its lord is posited there together with exalted Jupiter, which is significator for the 5th house. House, karaka (significator) and its lord, all are under the frustrating and delayed rays of exalted but retrograde Saturn. The power to delay becomes more prominent as Saturn is most powerful. Retrograde Saturn is also the lord of the 12th house. Thus there was delay in getting progeny. From the 9th house, we screen the preceptor, the lord of the 9th house Mars is exalted which shows that his preceptor should be knowledgeable. The qualities further increase on account of aspect of two natural benefics Moon, Jupiter to Mars. There is mutual aspect of Ketu and Jupiter. Dasarath had to perform the rituals and had to take the help of the divine power through Mantra Shakti. The 7th lord Mercury is under the influence of secretive Rahu and Rahu is posited in the 7th house. The significator of the 7th house Venus is also under the influence of invisible Ketu. Jupiter is aspecting Venus and Ketu. Kaikae tried to crown her son with the malefide intentions and invoked a boon. Dasarath's own wife became instrumental in spoiling the peace of the family. Dasarath died of a heart attack. Thus is clear on account of aspect of powerful Saturn on Sun (Heart).

CHAPTER 15

Political Astrology

Will Comet Damage Jupiter?

(This article was published in the planets & Forecast when scientists were raising too much alarms over the collision of Comet with Jupiter).

Jupiter was one of the first object to be studied by Galilo in the year 1610. Galilo discovered four moons (satellite) which are known as Gaililion moons. They are Lo, Europa Ganeymade and Galisto.

Jupiter is giant amongst the planets. If the mass (weight) of the earth is to be assumed as, 1 the mass of the Jupiter with relation to earth is 317.89. As such. Its mass is 71 percent of the total mass of the planetary system. It has one and a half times the volume of all other planets combined. Its size is so big that thirteen earths can easily fit in it. As against the earth's density of 5.5 the density of Jupiter is 1.3 *i.e.* roughly one fourth of the earth's density.

R. Wildt. in 1934, proposed a model giving Jupiter a rocky 60,000 kilometer in diameter, overlaid an ice shell of 27,000 km thick, above which lay the hydrogen rich atmosphere. According to Ramsey's theory (1951), the

1,20,000 km. crore was composed of hydrogen, so compressed that it assumed the characteristic of a metal. This core was overlaid by an atmosphere of 8,000 km deep layer of ordinary solid hydrogen, above which came the atmosphere.

JD Anderson and W.B. Hubbard (USA) say, "There is a relatively small rocky core made of iron and silicates and at a tempreture of about 30,000 degree C. Around this a thick shell or liquid metalic hydrogen prevail. At about 46,000 km from the centre of the planet there is a sudden transition from liquid metallic hydrogen to liquid molecular hydrogen. Its temperature is assumed to be 11000 degrees C with a pressure about three million time that of earth's air at sea level. Above the liquid molecular hydrogen comes the gaseous atmosphere, which is about 1000 km deep. It is made of 82 percent hydrogen atmosphere, which is about 1000 km. deep, it is made of 82 percent hydrogen and 17 percent helium and one percent ammonia and methane. IT is on account of this, the density of Jupiter is one fourth of the earth's Methane and ammonia which are formed when hydrogen joins with carbon and nitrogen respectively are also present in the atmosphere.

Jupiter radiates 1.7 times more energy than it would do if it depended only upon radiation received from the Sun. All other planets draw from the Sun whatever energy they possess. Jupiter emits random bursts of intense radio energy at long wave length. It is the most powerful radio object in the solar system, next to sun. No other planet is known to possess radio energy of its own. The credit of first detection of radio radiation goes to B.F. Burke, F.L. Franklim of USA (1955).

Jupiter has 16 satellities Falieon satellites travel in circulation orbit around Jupiter. Four outmost satellites are much smaller and travel in irregular orbits. These revolve round Jupiter from East to West.

On March 5, 1979 Voyager I made its closets approach and continued its exploration for a month. Then Voyager 2 took over. Some of the interesting discoveries are :

(a)   Jupiter too has a ring system. They are thin, being only 30 kilometres thick.

(b)   Three more moons (satellites) were discovered, thus making the total to sixteen. Ganymade was found to be biggest satellite in the total of sixteen. Ganymade was found to be biggest satellite in the whole solar system with a radius of 2638 kilometers. It pushed Titan, the satellite of Saturn to second place.

(c)   The innermost satellite Lo is the most active. Voyagers saw all least & volcanos actually erupting.

(d)   Jupiter and LO are connected by a flux tube of eletrons and ions carrying a current of 5 million amperes.

(e)   The Jupiter atmosphere was found to consist of 89 precent hydrogen and 11 percent helium with smaller amount of other substances. Hydrogen compound include ammonia, water and ammonium hydro sulphide.

(f)   The Red spot was found to be in rotation in anticlokwise with a period of 12 days at its outer edge and 9 days somewhere inside.

The ring system of Jupiter was also discovered from voyager 1 there is in fact one major ring extending from between 1,22,000 and 129,000 km from the planet's centre. so that the reach to cover 50,000 km above the cloud tops. The magnetic field of Jupiter was found to be stronger than for any other planet.

Comet Shoe maker–Levy 9 was discovered by Shoe maker on March 23, 1993. After studying its orbit astronomers concluded that shoe maker levy-9 passed near Jupiter two years ago. The tidal forces of Jupiter split it into 21 major pieces. The largest piece is 4 km. The speed of comet is 160,000 KPH.

As the comet is much smaller, as such it will have hardly any effect on gigantic Jupiter because it will be a drop in the ocean.

TAMILNADU ELECTION

The Article appreared in May 2001 issue of the Planets & forecast, Cuttack

JAYALALITA

Born on 24-2-1948 Time : 14 : 34 hr Mysoor, The horoscope is as under:

Ven	Rahu	12	Asc	Ven	Rahu	12	Asc
Sun Merc. (R)	JANMA KUNDLI		Sat (R)	Sun Merc. (R)	JANMA KUNDLI		Sat (R)
8			Moon Mars (R)	8			Moon Mars (R)
Jup	6	Ketu	4	Jup	6	Ketu	4

It is tendency of retrograde planet that they give power to a person if they influence the 10th house, if the person is out of power and withdraw it when he is in power. In case of Jaya Lalita, there are three retrograde planets in her chart. Mercury is retrograde in the 9th house and Saturn is retrograde in 2nd house in Cancer. Retrograde Mars in Leo in 3rd house is aspecting the 10th house. In 1996 when the elections were held two planets Mercury & Jupiter were retrograde, Jupiter is lord of 10th house and it was retrograde at the time of election. She was out of power.

At present she is passing through the main period of Rahu sub-period of Saturn from 7-8-99 to 5-8-2002. She is passing sub-period of the Moon which shall end on 22-6-2001. At the time of election Mars hall be retrograde and aspecting the house of profession. It will bring her to power once again.

The horoscope of **AIDMK** is as under:

The 10th lord is retrograde. This means that the party will come to power once again. At presxent AIDMK is passing through the main-period of Jupiter and sub-period of Saturn who is retrograde in natal chart and is aspecting the 10th house as a Yogakaraka planet it will bring the party in power.

11	12	Asc Sat	Ketu
10	**17.10.1972** **JANAM** **KUNDLI**		3
Moon			Ven
Jup Rahu	7	Sun Mer	Mars

Asc Mer	2	3	Jup K Mar
12	**NAVAMSA**		4
11			Moon
Rahu	9	Ven Sun	Sat

KARUNA NIDHI

The horoscope of Karuna Nidhi is as under:

9	Mer	Asc Sat	Ven
Ketu	**JANAM** **KUNDLI**		Asc
Mars			Rahu
6	Jup (R)	Sat (R)	3

4	Rahu	Ven Mer	Sun
3	**NAVAMSA**		8
Jup			Moon
Asc	Sat.	Ketu	Mars

His Saturn is posited in the 4th house and his Jupiter in the 5th house. Both are retrograde. At the time of election in 1996 Jupiter was retrograde which brought him to power. At present he is passing through the main period of Ketu and sub-period of Venus.

The retrograde planet has a peculiar tendency. They bring a person to power first time and next time. they render him powerless Saturn is in the 4th house aspecting the 10th house. It indicates that he will be out of power this time. The 10th Mars shall also be retrograde at the time of election which will show exit. The sub-period of Venus is in operation Venus is posited in the house of loss both in natal chart and navamsa chart. As such the stars are not in his favour.

(Jayalalitha came to power again.)

Will AGP Come to Power

The article appeared in June 2001 issue of the Planets & Forecast, Cuttack

Sun	9	Jup	Rahu
Mer			12
	CHART-1		
6			Asc
Moon	Mars	3	2

We do not have the horoscope of AGP. As such we shall make use of Horary Astrology Sh. Arun Gupta, One of the student put the query, "Will AGP come to power again?" The quey was raised on 17-3-2001.

The ascendant rules AGP. The ascendant lord Sun is ill placed in the 8th house. The 10th lord Venus is also placed in the 8th house. The placement of the 10th lord in the 6th, 8th or 12th house causes Duryoga. It means that AGP will not be able to come to power. At the time of election Mars shall be retrograde. This means that there will be opposition of the Chief Minister within its party and there may be open rift in the party. This will damage the presetige of the party.

We judge opposition from the 7th house so the lord of 7th house is considered as Ascendant here. The ascendant lord Saturn is posited in the 4th house aspecting the ascendant and the tenth house. The tenth lord Mars is posited in the tenth house.

Mars shall be retrograde at the time of election. It is peculiarity of the retrograde planet that it reverse the present action. The lord of the opposition, Sun is posited in the second house with retrograde Venus. It means that the break away group may join the Congress. At present congress is not in power. It will come to power.

(AGP) lost and Congress came to power in Assam)

Let us see if 'Sh. Buddadev will continue in power in West Bengal? 5:55 hours Noida 21-3-2001.

The ascendant lord Jupiter is very well placed in the third house and aspecting the house of fortune. Moon the lord of the house of competition is aspecting its own house. It is favourable situation for the party in power. In the ascendant, the sun who is the lord of the house of secret enemy and Venus who is lord of the 8th house do not favour. This indicates that the secret enemy will damage the party and there will be too much tilt in the behaviour pattern of the voters. The tenth lord is also Jupiter. As such he will continue in power.

Asc Sun Ven (R)	2	Jup Sat	Rahu
Mer			5
Moon	CHART-1		6
Ketu	Mars	8	7

The lord of the opposition is Mercury which is placed in the 12th hosue. It is also lord of the tenth house. The placement of the tenth lord in the 12th house causes duryoga and indicates loss of power. The bickerings in the opposition, who will try to combine, will continue and they will try to damage themselves.

(There was rift in Trimool Congress. Congress candidates also did not support from their heart. Sh. Buddadev continued as Chief Minister.)

SH. ATAL BIHARI VAJPAYEE

The article appeared in April-98 Issue of the

Planets & forecast Cuttack

The horoscope discussion is as under:

The yogakaraka Saturn is exalted in the ascendant and aspecting the 10th house. True to the quality of Saturn, the person will satrt his career at a lower level and will continue to rise to the zenith by his hard work. Such persons are always self made. The ascendant lord Venus is well placed but is in between Sun and Saturn and so is hemmed in the house of family. The 10th lord Venus. This amounts to a very powerful Rajyoga but as the Moon is debilitated, he will start his career from a lower position. Debilitated Moon is in the house of speech and aspected by Rahu makes him to use over power reasoning and overflow eloquence which makes him politically shrewd.

Jupiter, the planet of religion and patriotism, is well placed in its own house and influencing the house of religion, father, foreign and fortune. This means that there will be continuous development. There is association of 9th lord Mercury with the 11th lord Sun with the lord Jupiter. The association of

6 Mer	7	8	9
5	JANAM KUNDLI		Rahu
Ketu			11
Jup Mer Sun	Ven Moon	Sat Asc	12

Jupiter and Mercury tunes him intellectually stimulating faculties of pleasant satire and critical comment to perfection. He will always be admired for his oratorial skill and compels audience to listen attentively. It also reflects that integrity need not be sacrificed at the altar of politics. There will be sincerity of words and deeds. Sun association means that the speech will also be related to politics but there will be blend of partriotism also. Such a powerful combination under the influence of Saturn who represents the violet rays which has shortest wavalength amongst the visible spectrum. Sun is the planet of fame and on account of aspect of the powerful Saturn, such persons can be imprisoned on account of political reasons.

The fifth house is also hemmed like the second house. There is influence of Rahu on the ascendant lord Venus and the tenth lord Moon, which makes him stateman at per excellence.

The seventh lord Mars is not only ill placed but also under the influence of Rahu. As such, all the factors involving family, children and wife are weak. The influence of seventh lord Mars on the yogakaraka Saturn is also a powerful Rajyoga.

Venus period commenced from May 1941. He joined RSS in that period on account of influence of Rahu on the ascendant lord and later on became member of Indian National Congress and was imprisoned on account of taking part in "Quit India Movement" and later on he stepped into the shoes of Shyam Prasad Mukheree. Hemmed Venus aspected by Rahu and influence of powerful Saturn on Sun is the root cause of it. He was again arrested alongwith other leaders and kept in custody during the entire period of Mrs. Indira Gandhi emergency. At that time also, he was passing through the sub period of Venus in the major period of Moon from March 75. Venus sub-period commenced from end Nov. 95 and he became Prime Minister of India in May 96 but could not retain it. Venus sub-period in the major period of Rahu will end in Nov. 98.

Shri Atal's first formal induction into party coincided with the launch of Jan Sangh at the time of 1951 elections when he was passing through the sub-period of Rahu in the Major period of Venus. In 1953 when Mrs.Vijaya Laxmi was sent as Ambassador, he contested in by election and was defeated. At that time, he was passing through sub-period of Jupiter in the major period of Venus March 1954.

Jupiter is severely obstructed by the powerful rays of exalted Saturn. He was placed in second position. Saturn did not allow Jupiter to play well but allowed him to join the Parliament at its fag end in April 57 when was fielded from three constituencies. He was declared elected in Lucknow. He was also elected from Balarampur and lost his deposit in Mathura. He was again elected in 1991 in Saturn sub-period and the major period of Rahu which ended in April 1992.

He lost from Balarampur constituency in the election held in March 1962. At that time, he was passing through sub-period of Mars in the major period of Sun. Sun is afflicted by powerful Saturn and Mars is not only ill placed but aspected by Rahu. Sun's main period on account of influence of powerful Saturn was not good. But on 4-3-1967, at the fag end of sub-period of Venus in the main period of Sun, he was again elected as Member of Parliament.

Again in the main period of Moon and the sub-period of Jupiter, he was elected to Lok Sabha in 1971. He was elected in March 1977, when he was passing through the sub-period of Sun in the major period of Moon which was upto may 1977.

He became President of Jan Sangh in Feb. 68 in Moon-Moon period which ended in March 68 and retained it for three sucessive terms. He was elected to Lok Sabha in March 1977 and was External Affairs Minister till the end of Dec. 1979. He was re-elected in January 1980. At that time he was passing through the sub-period of Mercury in the major period of Mars. His main period of Rahu commenced from May 1984 and he could not enter the Lok Sabha on account of influence of Rahu on the ascendant lord Venus. But he was elected to Rajya Sabha at feg end of Rahu-Rahu in 1986.

His strong Mercury aspecting the house of foreign land helped him to meet foreign dignitaries as Pt. Nehru used to introduced to him to foreign dignitaries and once told to the Prime Minister of UK. "He is a member of opposition but a day will come, when he will become a great leader.

CHAPTER 16

Sub-Sub-Period and Transit

The article appeared in Annual issue 1997 of Babaji
The interpretation of the horoscope is a foundation on which the presitge of the astrology depends. While interpreting and reviewing the horoscope, the sub-sub period provides a clue as to what will happen to individual. The accuracy of the prediction will become more refined. If we see that what will be the situation of the planets which is sub sub lord in the transit. An attempt had been made in this article to indicate the role of sub sub lord with the transit of that particular planet. Suppose the sub sub period is Venus, in that case we have to check the position of Venus during that period. Stress in this article is laid on above and author's view are that this is the basis to pin point any interets of a horoscope. Let us discuss some horoscopes:

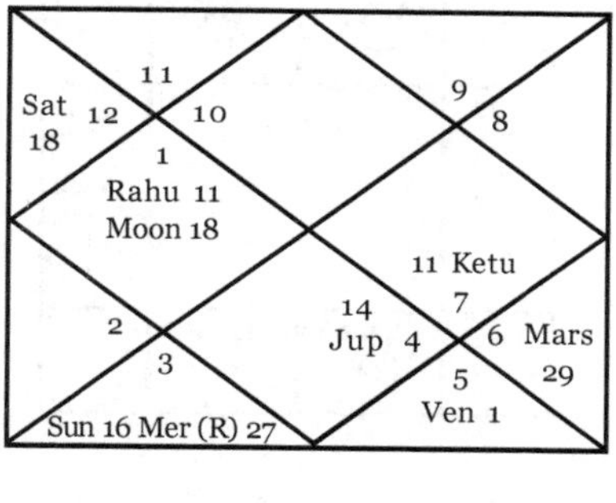

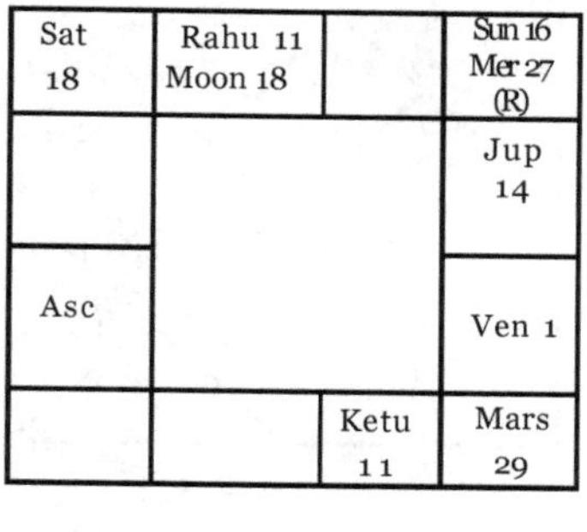

Chart 1 (North Indian):
```
            11
  Sat  12      10        9
  18                          8
       1
    Rahu 11
    Moon 18
                     11 Ketu
                14      7
     2         Jup 4      6 Mars
        3                5    29
  Sun 16 Mer (R) 27   Ven 1
```

Chart 2 (South Indian):

Sat 18	Rahu 11 Moon 18		Sun 16 Mer 27 (R)
			Jup 14
Asc			Ven 1
		Ketu 11	Mars 29

His Venus sub period in the major period of Moon commenced from 18.1.1994. Venus is ill placed and the placement of the 10th lord in the 6th, 8th or the 12th house caused the duryoga and the person lost his job.

On 13.2.94 Sun shifted to Aquarius. The planetary position at that Time was as under:

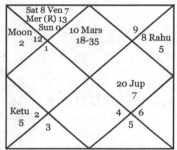

Moon 2	Rahu 11 Moon 18		
Sat 8 Mer 3 Sun 0 Ven 7			
Mars 18-35 Asc			
	Rahu 5	Jup 20	

Mercury retrograde from 11.2.94. Mercury in the main chart is retrograde Mercury is the lord of the house of fortune and is powerfully placed in its own house. The sub sub-period of Venus commenced from 18.1.94. During this period a complete disharmony occurred between him ans his boss. Venus in the main is ill placed and it was very close to Saturn 8 dergee and the Venus longitude is one became combust from February 8 and remained combust upto 13.3.94. He resigned before Sun left Aquarius on 14.3.94.

There was a hue and cry in the family on account of this resignation. He appeared in an interview and was selected. He got the appointment letter and they decided to celebrate this by visiting to a hill station.

He joined the new on 1.4.94 the planetary position was as under:

Sun 17	Venus 5	Ketu 1	
Sat 13 Mars 25 Sun 0 Mer 22 Asc			
	Rahu 1 Moon 19	Jup (R) 19/23	

Jupiter retrograded from 28-2-94 and was in the house of profession and indicated the change of the job. Venus shifted to Aries on 28-3-94 and aspected the house of prefession. He got the job was not allowed to join and was told on 1-4-94, with commencement of the month. There are two salient feature *(i)* Moon is debilitated on the date of joining and *(ii)* Jupiter is retrograde aspecting the lord of the 10th house. This indicates that he may leave this job and join some other concern.

He was not satisfied and was in search of an alternative job. He joined another firm in 1.8.94. The planetary position of that time was as under:

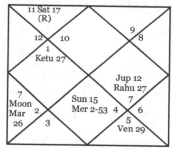

	Ketu 27	Moon 7 Mars 26	
Sat 17 (R)			Sun 15 Mer 3
Asc			Ven 29
		Jup 12 Rahu 27	

Sub sub-period of Moon is closely associated with Rahu and is influencing the house of profession. As such there was no job satisfaction. At the time of submitting the resignation Venus was ill placed in the 8th house on the next day. Jupiter is posited in house of profession. The ascendant lord Saturn is retrograde and there is no influence of retrograde. Saturn in the house of fortune or prefession. As such there will be continuity in the service. his sub-sub-period of Moon ended on 19.7.94 and Mars periods commenced. Mars sub sub-period upto 28.8.94 and the transit Mars was well placed in the 5th house.

Het got married on 20.1.95 in the sub sub-period of Jupiter, Jupiter is posited in the 7th house and is exalted.

His wife is M.Sc. and is a lecturer in some college in Delhi. The planetary position on 20.1.95 was as under:

The sub sub lords is Jupiter in the main chart. It is exalted and posited in the 7th house and aspecting the lord of the second house. In trasit Jupiter is posited in the 11th house and aspecting the house of marriage. It is associated with the Venus, the significator for marriage, The sub sub lord Jupiter and the significator Venus are aspected by Saturn, the ascendant lord.

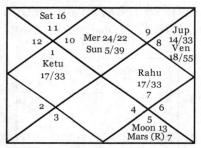

Let us discuss an another case : 8-4-1972 Delhi 14-10

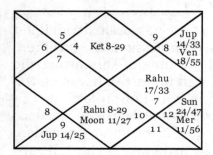

Ketu afflicted Sun and retrograde Mercury. Rahu is afflicting Moon very closely. This will make the person very sensitive and he will immediately feel frustrated. Rahu closely afflicted Venus, Saturn and Mars. He joined MBA classes in New Delhi.

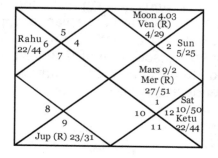

Ketu 11-20 Ven 24-26	Sun 16-16 Mer (R) 22-34	Moon 14-37
Sat 16		Ascdt.
		Mars 9-08
	Jup 16-47	Rahu 11-20

He was sent to a Bank for training in Delhi. The bank assigned a job in New Delhi and by the time he could join, Mercury became retrograde. He was asked to proceed to Kanpur and he had to visit one factory after another. At that not only the climatic conditions were very bad but also there was communal disharmony. The planetary position as on 1.6.95 when he was asked to visit Kanpur for a period of two months was as under:

Mercury became retrograde on 24-5.95 and there was a change in the decision of the management and he was posted to Kanpur. In the natal chart Rahu is influencing Venus, Saturn and Mars. At the time of the event Rahu was influencing Saturn and Ketu influenced Mars and Venus, Mercury was retrograde in both the cases.

Sat Ketu	Mer (R) 27-51 Mar 9.02	Sun 5-27	Ven 4-29 Moon 4-03
			Ascdt
jup (R) 23-31			Rahu 23

He was passing through the sub sub-period of Mercury in the sub period of Mercury and major period of Rahu from 19.2.96 Mercury became retrograde from 5.5.96, Mars is very well placed in the house of prfession. His Mercury in the natal is retrograde and is associated with Sun and aspected by Ketu. He joined the Bombay region in a foreign company. The degree is Mercury (R) is 12 and the degree of Ketu is 9. There is a close aspect of Ketu on Mercury. At the time of joining, Sun was very well placed and aspected by Saturn which indicates that the superior officer will get annoyed for no fault of the person. Moon is ill placed Saturn is in the 9th house and is indicating the western region. Retrograde Jupiter is sub sub-period and Transit.

Aspecting the 2nd house and it indicates departure from the family.

Let us discuss an another case.

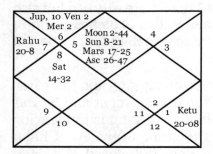

	Ketu 20-08		
			Ascdt
			Asc 26-47 Moon 2-44 Mar 17-25
	Sat 14-32	Rahu 20-08	Jup 10-08 Ven 12-48 Mer 1-47

The 10th lord Venus was debilitated and was hemmed in between Mars and Rahu The second house representing family and wealth was also ascendant and the ascendant lord Sun and the 9th lord Mars. It amounts to a very powerful Yoga on account of the association of 10th lord Venus and 2nd and 11th lord Mercury and the 5th Jupiter. But this yoga has been rendered weak on account of hemming.

Let us analyse the 10th house of the chart. He joined an aviation company on 13.4.1989. The planetary position on 13.4.1989 was as under:

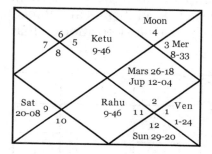

Sub sub-period of Moon in the main period of Moon commenced from 19.3.89. There was exchange of the lords of 9th house and the 10th house and association of lords of house and the 5th house at the time of the appointment. The 7th lord Saturn was also very well placed. He worked for for more than five years and then resigned from this company and joined another on 1.8.1994.

The sub sub period of Mars in the Sub-period of Saturn and the major period of Moon ended on 7.8.94. The planetary position on 1.8.94 when in this new company was as under:

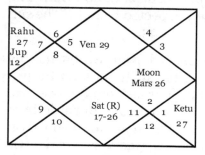

The retrograde Saturn in transit aspected the house of fortune and the 10th lord Venus. The 9th lord Mars was in the house together with Moon, the planet of change.

The ascendant lord was ill placed and the 10th lord Venus 29 was closely aspected by Ketu 27. All these factors indicated that adverse period was ahead. His sub sub period Rahu ended on 3.11.94 followed by Jupiter which ended on 17.1.95. He left the job in the last week of December 94 and joined another company on 3.1.95. The planetary position on that date was as under :

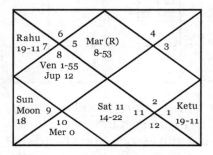

	Ketu 19-11		
Sat 14-22			
Mer 0			Mar (R) 8-53 Asc
Sun 9 Moon 18	Ven 1-55 Jup 12	Rahu 19-11	

Mars retrograde on 3.1.95 as lord of the 9th house. At the time of previous appointment there was influence of retrograde Saturn on the house of fortune and the 9th lord Venus was closely aspected by Ketu. In this case the 10th lord was Venus and aspected the 10th house but retrograde Mars aspected the 10th lord Venus though aspected its own house but was hemmed in between Rahu and Sun. The ascendant lord Sun was closely aspected by Ketu. The sub sub period of Jupiter ended on 17.1.95.

Mercury sub period commenced from 18.1.95 and the sub sub period of Sun ended on 21.8.95 In the natal Saturn aspected and in August 1995 Sun in transit opposed Saturn. The management withdraw the work from him and there too much humiliation. Sub sub-period of Moon ended on 3.10.95. Moon in the natal chart was very weak. His humiliation further aggravated and there was too much depression. The natal chart Saturn 15° aspected Mars 17° and also Ketu 19° aspected Mars. Mars was retrograde when he joined this concern Sun, the ascendant lord was also under the grip of Ketu very closely, Rahu's Sub sub-period was from 2.11.95 to 19.1.96 He was jobless during Rahu's Sub sub-period. The planetary position on 30.10.95 was as under:

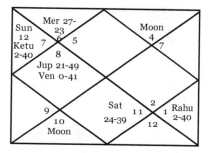

	Rahu 2-40		
Sat 24-39			
Moon			Asc
Jup 21-49 Mar 12-46 Ven 00-41	Sun 12 Ketu 2-40	Mer 27-33	

The ascendant lord Sun was ill placed. The 10th lord Venus was not only ill placed with Rahu also, Mars the lord of the fortune was also posited in the 6th house though exalted but was combust and aspected its own house. He had to resign on 22.3.96 but the company agreed to pay him salary upto 30.4.96. He joined another concern, The planetary positions on 7.2.96 and 10.4.96 were as under:

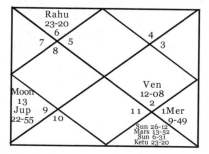

Sun 26-36 Mar 13-52 Sat 6-31 Ketu 23-20	Mer 9-49	Ven 12-08	
			Asc
Moon 13 Jup 22-55			Rahu 23-20

There is an association of the lord ascendant and the 7th lord Saturn and the 9th lord Mars, Saturn represented his wife who had to resign and he had to spend money on the shifting of the house from New Delhi to Bombay. His sub period of Saturn ended on 18.6.96. As such during sub sub-period of Saturn he had to suffer finacnial losses on account of placement of the Saturn in the 8th house.

CHAPTER **17**

Astral Remedies

A strology without remedies is like a body without a soul. The body is useless without a soul. In the same way, there is limited use of astrology, if we are not able to mitigate our problems with the help of astral remedies.

Sage Parasar, the founder of the astrology had assigned several chapters on Astral remedies in his works. He studied the effects of stars/planets on animate and inanimate objects and after studying the wavelength of each products he prescribed way to control the rays of the planets. There are various ways which help us in mitigation as astral miseries. These are charity, yantras, fasting, mantra citation. Of late, gems therapy, colour therapy and use of roots and herbs has gained wide curency.

Charity

Charity is the most invaluable weapon against the effects of planets. Our rishis who were scientists of lure were able to eastablish wavelengths of each and very product including cereals. Modern science has also worked out the wavelength of all metals, gems etc. By donating products ruled by different planets a person can repel the rays which harm

156 of Astrology Everybody Must Know

him at a particular time. This has been explained in detail in author's other book. Briefly the products ruled by each planet have been included. These may be distributed to needy persons and/or charitable homes and those Ashrams where Sadhus live. Sub consciously the receiver who uses these products, blesses the donor and thereby the donor is relieved of his problems. In addition to this, as a routine, we may feed bread, sweet, salted or plain to animals and birds. THE LAW OF NATURE IS THAT PEOPLE WHO DONATE MORE AND MORE, GET BACK NOT ONLY RETURN IN MATERIAL FORM BUT ALSO RELIEF FROM THEIR PROBLEMS. We all know that if we sow 5 kg of wheat, we get 50 kg. of wheat, but we have to sow first and reap later on. Abdul Rahim Khankhana, the royal astrologer to the king Akbar had advocated the necessity of charity. He goes to the extent of saying "Rahiman vay nar mar chuke jo hein magan jahni, tin se pehale vay mare hoot karat hein nahi". According to him, those people who asks for alms are treated as dead persons, but they (donor) die earlier than such persons, if they have the resources but they decline to offer something to the needy.

Yantra

Yantra is also to be profitably used to strengthen the weak planets. The Yantra of each planet is as under, But before it is explained, we must know that there are 27 constellations.

They are:

Constellations	Ruler of the consellation	Years alloted in main period	Metal	Yantra No. alloted to the planet
1	2	3	4	5
Aswani Magha Mool	Ketu	7	Steel	39
Bharani, P. Phalguni, P. Sadha	Venus	20	Platinum	30
Kritika, U. Phalguni U. Sadha	Sun	6	Copper	15
Rohini, Hasia, Sravana	Moon	10	Silver	18
Mrgsira, Chitra, Dhanista	Mars	7	Copper	21
Ardra Swati, Satabhisa	Rahu	18	Steel	36
Pvasu, Visaka, P. Bhadrapada	Jupiter	16	Gold	27
Pusya Anuradha, U. Bhadrapada	Saturn	19	Steel	33
Aslesa, Jyestha Revati	Mercury	17	Bronze	24

Rationlaity add three everytime. Sun 15, Moon 18, Mars 21, Mercury 24, Jupiter 27, Venus 30, Saturn 33, Rahu 36 and Ketu 39. The individual yantra is to be engraved on the relevent metal on a day when Moon transits the constellation ruled by the planet and it should be worn on that particular day. On that day the planet is powerful as it rules the particular constellation.

The Yantras of different planets are us under:

SUN

6	1	8
7	5	3
2	9	4

MOON

7	2	9
8	6	4
3	10	5

MARS

8	3	10
9	7	5
4	11	6

MERCUIRY

9	4	11
10	5	8
5	12	7

JUPITER

10	5	12
11	9	7
6	13	8

MARS

11	6	13
12	10	8
7	14	9

SATURN

12	7	14
13	11	9
8	15	10

RAHU

13	8	15
14	12	10
9	16	11

KETU

14	9	16
15	13	11
10	17	12

Fasting

The most effective weapon to repel/control the wavelength of a particular planet can be with the help of fasting. Propitiation of a planet can be done by fasting on the day ruled by that planet. If more than two planets are afflicting the native, he will have to fast for several days which will definitally affect his health. To avoid such a situation we recommend fasting a particular God instead of the fasting for a particular planet. Normally we recommend for Tuesday. The equivalent word in Devnagari script is Mangal which means auspicious. So, Tuesday is an auspicious day for fasting. During fasting we recommend:

(a) To take a glass of milk in the morning.

(b) To drink as much water as possible.

(c) To take different types of fruit & vegetables in the evening without salts/spices.

(d) To recite Hanuman chalisa either in the morning or in the evening.

The fasting had a dual effect. It gives rest to our stomach who stores energy for our future requirement and it control the ill effect of the planets. Fasting neutralises the blood pressure of the individual. Ladies can keep fast on Tuesdays. Thousands of ladies kept fast on Tuesday under our supervision and all were benefitted. It should be noted that ladies worship Sh. Hanuman as a divine deity & as such he helps such ladies as a father takes care of his children.

Christian can fast on Sundays. Those Muslims who fast during Ramzan need not fast on a weekly basis. It is necessary that those who do not have adverse period may fast regularly as it will maintain good health and keep the extra energy for future reprelling of effect of the planets.

Roots & Herbs

Indian scientist worked out the wavelength of each and every product and those who could not afford charity were advised to take bath in different types of roots or herbs. They modified the scientific system in a layman language and gave it a religious sanctity in order to enable a person to repreat these off and on. They treated the planets as a particular deity so that people may propititate them and may not feel them as merely the planets.

In fact their purpose was that the people may perform these remedies and be benefitted. Taking bath with these medicinal plants brings about a particular odour and aroma which suits the particular planet. Our sages had discovered that each planet apart from emitting rays and light also emits a certain type of aroma. Taking bath with medicinal plants creates that type of aroma which is congenial to the aroma of the planet which is sought to be propitiated. The planetary herbs are as under:

Sun	Saffron, lotus and cardamom
Moon	Pearl, conch shell. lotus betel, leaves and rice
Mars	Red flower, red sandal, brinjal roots
Mercury	Honey
Jupiter	Yellow mustard seeds, yellow flower
Venus	White Lotus, silver
Saturn	Mustard oil, antimony, sea-same

Any one of product of a particular planet may be used for bathing. This will be as effective as other measures.